The Daily Proverbs

*365 Devotional Sayings on
How to Live a Better Life*

By

R.W. Reese

Dedicated to my Mom and Dad, for without your support, I wouldn't be where I am today.

Introduction

I want to make it clear that I didn't attend church every Sunday growing up. I didn't go to Bible school. I didn't read the Bible cover to cover when I was younger. Sure, I would go to the occasional church service with my family, mostly around the holidays but that was about it. Instead, I got swept away with trying to be a cool teenager that was indifferent toward any spiritually uplifting activities. I always believed in God, but never sought him out on a consistent basis. Instead, I focused more on my own ego.

Throughout my twenties, I devoted my entire being to gaining status in the corporate world. I was always seeking the next promotion or bonus at any cost. I'd spend money on flashy purchases that only made the void grow bigger within me. It was at the expense of my time for friends and family and my relationship with God. That was all until one day, I had a spiritual awakening. When looking to break free from my self-destructive behavior, I kept seeing a consistent theme among the literature I was reading: "surrender to a higher being," the messages wrote. But without direction and purpose in my life, I wasn't sure who or what to surrender to.

My twenties had flashed before me in the blink of an eye. Was I really going to spend my entire life like this? I was doing the same things over and over each day but expecting different results. Until one day, at a low point, I downloaded one of the Bible apps on my phone. I wasn't expecting much from it, I was merely seeking an occasional verse or passage I could relate to. I found myself picking it up and reading more of it each morning. I kept going back to the proverbs and finding meaning in each one. Slowly but surely, my life was improving. My relationship with God was blossoming. The void within me was closing. My bad habits faded away into the abyss like a sun setting in the distance. It wasn't an overnight change. It happened from consistency. It took me surrendering to God and asking to be forgiven before religion truly found me. My life had light again.

I wrote this book to share some of what I learned and included the proverbs (NLV translations) that most helped me find meaning in life.

January 1st

*"Listen, my son, to your father's instruction and
do not forsake your mother's teaching."*

PROVERBS 1:8

Godly parents are a gift from God. Their guidance, wisdom, and direction are an extension of the Lord's providence in our lives. We must submit ourselves to our parents' teachings and let them draw us ever closer to the Lord. Our father's give logical advice and our mother's set a good example for us. Think back to some of their greatest teachings and ask yourself, am I living each day with their intentions in mind?

January 2nd

"A man without self-control is like a city broken into and left without walls."

PROVERBS 25:28

The lack of discipline in life could lead to eventual despair. Ask God for forgiveness and continue to follow in his faith. Surrender your addictions or bad habits to his higher power and watch your life transform. Whether it's social media, substances, or adult content, attempt to limit your desires and keep things to moderation. God will forgive us, but we must commit to following His faith to build our own personal "city" walls high and mighty. The more self-discipline we have in life, the more time we will have for creating healthy habits: exercise, reading, and spending time with friends and family.

January 3rd

"The wages of the righteous is life, but the earnings of the wicked are sin and death."

PROVERBS 10:16

We will reap what we sow. It's a clichéd saying, but it's true! When we focus our lives on godly pursuits, we will enjoy the blessings of God. When we turn from Him and give our lives over to sin, we walk a self-destructive path of our own making. Find the balance between holy living and devotional pursuits. The more we follow living in righteousness, the more abundance we can attract into our lives. Abundance could come in the form of relationships, financial freedom, or good health. Whichever we seek, we should be conscious of having pure intentions and avoiding sin.

January 4ᵗʰ

"A false witness will not go unpunished, and whoever pours out lies will not go free."

PROVERBS 19:5

God loves an honest heart, and He likewise despises lies. Why is that? Lies hurt others, plain and simple. Our God is a God of truth, love, and peace. Lies go against each of those things. They are contrary to the will of God! We must devote ourselves to honesty in every situation, no matter the cost. Sometimes the truth may hurt. But lying stings much worse. Consider the foundation you are building in your relationships. A strong foundation is built on honesty and trustworthiness. Even if it feels uncomfortable, practice telling the truth in all situations without worrying about how others will respond.

January 5th

"The wise inherit honor, but fools get only shame."

PROVERBS 3:35

Wisdom comes straight from God Himself. He will guide us in every aspect of our lives. When we embrace worldly wisdom instead of the Lord's, we become fools. We must stand in the wisdom of God to thrive in every area of our lives! The wisdom of God can guide us out of the darkest depths. His wisdom is the light at the end of a long tunnel. Turn to him and ask for clarity. Tune out the surrounding noise of the constant negativity from the news, whose aim is to stoke fear. You will find what you seek. The beginning of every new journey starts with God.

January 6th

"Fools mock at making amends for sin, but goodwill is found among the upright."

PROVERBS 14:9

We will all sin in life, no matter how closely we walk to the Lord. But that's okay! What's important is that we come to Him with a repentant heart. Our downfall will come when we are unrepentant for our sins and continue in them. It takes a wise and courageous heart to confess our sins, but that's where we'll find true growth! God is forgiving. We mustn't be scared to ask for help. Start by being more aware of how your actions are affecting yourself and others. If you notice some of these actions or habits may be sinful, open your heart and ask God to forgive you. The first step is letting go of our ego.

January 7th

"Drink water from your own cistern, running water from your own well."

PROVERBS 5:15

This verse speaks to sexual morality. God has created sex to be expressed between a married man and woman alone. When we are enticed by random sexual partners or even adult content, we disregard God's design for what's meant to be a holy act. The concept may seem outdated in the modern world. It may even be difficult to follow, but it's the intention that is key. Keep God's wish for us in mind and try your best to conform to it when able to live your truest life. Don't be hard on yourself if you can't always adhere to it, we are all sinners in our own way. Ask to be forgiven and attempt to do better in the future.

.

January 8th

"Without wood a fire goes out; without a gossip a quarrel dies down."

PROVERBS 26:20

Our God is a God of peace. As His children, He calls us to lives of peace as well. Gossip is the enemy of peace. We are only to say kind, encouraging, or empowering words to others. If we can't find any of those to say, then it's better we don't speak at all. Practice self-control when it comes to speaking about others. Pretend they were in the room with you. If they were, would you still speak the same words? We all have emotions, and sometimes they overpower us. But, if we can stop and take a deep breath first, we're more likely to say something positive and encouraging that can defuse a situation.

January 9th

"The fear of the LORD leads to life; then one rests content, untouched by trouble."

PROVERBS 19:23

There is healthy and unhealthy fear. Healthy fear is respect and reverence for the Lord that leads to trust in Him and great faith. Unhealthy fear breeds worry in our hearts and leads us away from peace in God. Choose godly fear and build your trust in His loving guidance and power. When first adopting the concept of fearing God, you may find yourself overthinking situations. You might ask yourself: would God approve of this? Be conscious of this thought and try to stay present in the moment. The more you sit with the fear of the Lord, the clearer your intended path will become.

January 10th

*"In the way of righteousness there is life; along
that path is immortality."*

PROVERBS 12:28

The good and loving acts we commit toward others have a
lasting impact greater than we could ever know. A single act
of godly kindness can reflect the love of Jesus toward others and
change someone's life forever. Commit to modeling your life
after Jesus in every way. Ask yourself: would Jesus lend a helping
hand? Would he give to those in need? Perhaps it's something
small like in the form of leaving a larger tip at a restaurant or
helping someone move into a new home. Extend yourself to
others and righteousness will be found. The less we focus on
ourselves, the freer we become.

January 11th

"Keep my commands and you will live; guard my teachings as the apple of your eye."

PROVERBS 7:2

God doesn't want us to follow His teachings out of obligation or blind obedience. He desires that we would come to love His truth and genuinely desire to follow it. He wants us to build our lives upon the foundation of His truth and walk in His ways with joy. Maybe you just found religion, or it found you. Perhaps you're a lifelong devotee. Whichever the case, you decided to pick up this book. Not out of requirement, but out of the curiosity to learn more. Stick with it. Try to live each day with gratitude by thanking God for all the blessings we have in life.

January 12th

*"Love prospers when a fault is forgiven, but
dwelling on it separates close friends."*

PROVERBS 17:9

Forgiveness is at the heart of our faith. Jesus brought us
forgiveness through His sacrifice on the cross, and we are
called to practice it as well. When we do, we become more like
Jesus and fulfill the will of God for our lives. Not forgiving
destroys relationships and pulls us further away from God.
Think of a time someone has wronged you. Do you wish the
relationship or friendship could have been saved? Maybe it was
an honest mistake, we all make those. Start by forgiving
something small and see how you feel. The more we practice
forgiveness, the easier it gets over time.

January 13th

"Whoever stubbornly refuses to accept criticism will suddenly be destroyed beyond recovery."

PROVERBS 29:1

The Bible can't stress enough the importance of being coachable. When we are dead set in our beliefs and refuse to be guided by God's truth, pride quickly fills our hearts. That pride leads to our downfall in every way. We must cast it aside and be molded by God's truth. Put your ego aside and be able to laugh at yourself. Part of living a holier life is to accept that we aren't always right. Someone will always have greater knowledge of something than we do. Keep the curiosity to learn strong and your mind will blossom with new ideas.

January 14th

"The godly care about the rights of the poor; the wicked don't care at all."

PROVERBS 29:7

Jesus had a heart for the poor. There are numerous times throughout the Gospel when we see Him serving them and meeting their needs. He teaches His disciples the importance of it as well. Jesus wants us to serve and care for the poor, just as He did. Look for opportunities in your community to impact the lives of those in need. Whether you live in a big city or rural community, there will always be someone in need. Even if you don't have the means to help them financially, see if you can aid by lending your time. Keep those less fortunate in your prayers and remember that God loves everyone equally.

January 15th

"Wickedness never brings stability, but the godly have deep roots."

PROVERBS 12:3

If we want to find stability in life, all we must do is follow God's ways. His truth, found in the Holy Bible, teaches us the right way to live. When we go our own way, we are subject to a rollercoaster of problems brought about by our lifestyle. But when we live in godliness, we have deep roots that will continually guide us along stable paths. There are many distractions in the modern world that disrupt stability. Being on the rollercoaster of emotions may bring short-term happiness but can leave a bigger void within us long term. Seek a simpler, holier life.

January 16th

"A sensible person wins admiration, but a warped mind is despised."

Wisdom comes from the Lord! Even when it seems like the people around us don't hear or understand it, you can rest assured that godly wisdom will have its impact and eventually, it can win you respect from the right people. Do you ever feel like you can't get through to someone despite your best efforts? Are you having trouble seeing eye to eye with them on a particular topic? Try sticking to your moral ground and speak politely while respecting other people's viewpoints. Over time, your godly wisdom will shine brighter, and you will be admired for having a pure conscience.

January 17th

"The way of the righteous is like the first gleam of dawn, which shines ever brighter until the full light of day."

PROVERBS 4:18

Think of how the sun looks early in the morning. Its pure rays cast down on this beautiful planet that God created. Living a righteous life is a beautiful thing. The seemingly small changes that happen initially as we turn toward God, shift into brilliant and beautiful lights in our lives, like rays of early-morning sunshine. Righteous living has a way of multiplying the blessings in our lives as they impact not only our reality but the lives of those around us. When you start noticing improvements in your life, be sure to thank God. Gratitude goes a long way and the more we practice it, the greater our awareness becomes toward the blessings in our lives.

January 18th

"For the LORD sees clearly what a man does,
examining every path he takes."

PROVERBS 5:21

We must be careful how we live our lives. In the world we
live in, it's easy to get sucked into a life of sin and not
even realize it. But God sees everything we do and desires
nothing more than for us to turn our lives toward Him.
Continually learn more from the Bible and attempt to pattern
your life after its amazing truth. We all have setbacks or moments
of weakness. Use them as motivation and shed any guilt or shame
that may result from them. Ask God for His love and forgiveness.
He will listen. And He will use his wisdom to guide us back to
our intended paths.

January 19th

"Riches won't help on the day of judgment, but right living can save you from death."

PROVERBS 11:4

Many people in this life are focused on building up as much wealth as possible. While money is necessary to survive in the world we live in, we must be careful not to make it an idol in our lives. Ultimately, God provides for our every need, and we must trust in Him to care for us. People on social media will often flaunt their riches. There's no need to do so. Be thankful for what you are blessed with. Praise God for anything more that comes your way and help give to those less fortunate. It's not to say that we shouldn't spend money, but there's much more to experience in life than riches.

January 20th

"If you help the poor, you are lending to the LORD—and He will repay you!"

PROVERBS 19:17

Our God is a gracious and loving God, and He created us in His image! That means we are to be loving toward others, helping to meet their needs when the opportunity arises. When we use our time, energy, and resources to minister to the poor, we are pleasing God and will reap eternal rewards in heaven. Community plays a large role in life. In the modern age, community feels scarcer than ever before. Help lift those around you who are going through a tough time. Do unto others as you would hope someone would do unto you in a time of need. Strive to be a positive role model in your community.

January 21st

"Better to have little, with fear for the LORD,
than to have great treasure and inner turmoil."

PROVERBS 15:16

No amount of material possessions in this life will bring us true and lasting peace. There is only one place we can find eternal rest for our souls, and that is in the Lord! That's why it's crucial for us to shift our focus from the things of the world to the things of God. We all experience the desire for more in life from time to time. Whether it's the new car, a bigger house, or a cool piece of clothing. But in the process of constantly seeking more, we forget how blessed we already are. A good exercise to highlight this proverb is to try living beneath your means for a few months.

January 22nd

---

*"Anger is cruel, and wrath is like a flood, but
jealousy is even more dangerous."*

PROVERBS 27:4

In our world, it can be hard to find contentment. But that's only because we are looking in all the wrong places! We can find true contentment and peace only in our faith in Jesus. There, all jealousy, anger, and wrath in our hearts will cease to control us and we will be able to live in love and freedom. Anger and jealousy can fuel a life of sin. If you find yourself getting jealous over a partner, or someone who is deemed to have "more" than you, try and ask yourself why? What is it that we really fear? The same goes with anger. Instead of reacting to each of these emotions, simply be aware of when they arise. The first step toward being free from anger and jealousy is to acknowledge them.

January 23rd

*"Wounds from a sincere friend are better than
many kisses from an enemy."*

PROVERBS 27:6

Being a true friend is hard. Why? Because it can take brutal
and loving honesty that is challenging for most. But you
know what? It's always worth it. The advice and guidance of a
friend with godly wisdom is invaluable and can reset us on our
God-ordained path in life. Many people seek validation on social
media. Is this what the Lord intended for us? Will praise from a
mere stranger fill our hearts the way that a loved one can? It's
unlikely not to. Instead of chasing external validation, we can try
to foster validation from within. By loving ourselves, we will be
better friends and partners to those we love.

January 24th

---

*"By wisdom the LORD founded the earth; by
understanding He created the heavens."*

PROVERBS 3:19

Sometimes it can be easy to question God's direction in our
lives. When we can't see a particular outcome, we can have a
hard time walking in faith. But faith at its core means that we
don't have to see to believe. We can trust that the very power,
wisdom, and understanding that God used to create the world is
the very same that guides us through life when we walk with
Him. We need not understand every situation or conflict we are
faced with. But God can. Pray to Him and ask what He would
do. Let His wisdom clear a sacred path for you. When you follow
that path, you may unlock greater understanding of the world
that He's created for you.

January 25th

"Do not withhold good from those who deserve it when it's in your power to help them."

PROVERBS 3:27

God blesses our lives richly and gives us more than we even need. When we find ourselves in this situation, it means that God has granted us a powerful responsibility: to share our abundance for the benefit of others! That's exactly what God does in His ultimate love and power, and in this way, He calls us to follow His example. We can extend our helping hands to those who have helped us. We can start with small gestures to brighten someone's day. The positive intentions will make their way back to us one day, even if we aren't expecting anything in return.

January 26th

"Walk with the wise and become wise; associate with fools and get in trouble."

PROVERBS 13:20

The company we keep is crucial to the health of our personal growth. Surrounding ourselves with wise, godly people will help us to become wise and godly as well. But when we hang around people with unrepentant sin in their lives, we develop sinful habits too. Through prayer, ask for God's wisdom in choosing your inner circle! Think of coworkers, friends, family members or neighbors that leave you feeling drained. Sometimes others want to drag us down with them. Pay attention to those closest to you and if they have your best intentions at heart. If you feel like you are outgrowing some of your friends, it may be a sign that you're achieving significant personal growth.

January 27th

"Commit your actions to the LORD, and your plans will succeed."

PROVERBS 16:3

We can't do anything truly impactful without the help of the Lord. He is the author of every good thing in our lives. When we devote our lives and work to God, He will give us everything we need to not only succeed but thrive. Start your next venture or project with the Lord in mind. Seek to produce something that can have a positive impact on those around you. The journey will be fruitful. If we think less about the success of ourselves and more about helping others, we can find a higher purpose in our work. We'll wake up on a mission ready to make the most of each day.

January 28th

*"Commit yourself to instruction; listen carefully
to words of knowledge."*

PROVERBS 23:12

God's truth is what we must pattern our lives around. We must never fall for the trap of believing we have it all figured out. There is always more we can learn! That's why we must continually return to God's word and drink of its wisdom. When we do, we will grow in wisdom and faith daily. Carve out time to learn. Read some random passages or uplifting material instead of picking up the phone and endlessly scrolling. Seek additional knowledge and try to start producing something with your energy instead of consuming things.

January 29th

*"Wine produces mockers; alcohol leads to brawls.
Those led astray by drink cannot be wise."*

PROVERBS 20:1

Sadly, alcohol is far too often celebrated in our society. We use it as a means of social interaction and laugh when we abuse it and act foolish. It's time that we take it more seriously and realize we don't need alcohol to have fun or be social. It has the potential to create problems in our lives and lead us away from godly values. The occasional drink may not bring harm but be mindful of what things are said and done when consuming copious amounts of it. Would those words be said if we were sober, would we have acted that same way without alcohol? If we're in control of our vices, our minds and bodies can be in good condition for all situations.

January 30th

"The LORD directs our steps, so why try to understand everything along the way?"

In our modern, scientific age, we are so reliant upon information and facts that many of us have a hard time with faith. At times, it's challenging to believe in something that we cannot see. But faith means that we trust in God and don't need all the answers. With Him guiding our steps, we can find peace and contentment in the truth that all is in His hands, and we don't need to know everything along the way. Sometimes, less can be more. The less time we spend sitting around thinking, the more energy we have. Instead of overanalyzing something, try going with the flow and relinquish the control of needing to know everything.

January 31st

"Don't answer the foolish arguments of fools, or you will become as foolish as they are."

PROVERBS 26:4

One look at social media will show you just how much people will defend their opinions and thoughts on any given subject no matter how foolish they are. Then, as they argue further, they become more and more stubborn and foolish. We must avoid this tendency at all costs to prevent making the same mistakes. We must work towards peace with all and not engage in meaningless arguments. It's okay to have different views than someone else. But it's not worth the unrest that's created when arguing over them. Attempt to see beyond their views. Accept them for who they are and pray for them. The news, social media and political theater are meant to keep us distracted. Try paying less attention to the "fools" and more on what brings you joy in life.

February 1st

"*Wisdom will save you from the immoral woman, from the seductive words of the promiscuous woman.*"

PROVERBS 2:16

There are many temptations in this world that can draw us away from our faith if we are not careful. The pleasures of this world are many and the enemy will not hesitate to use them against us at any chance He gets. Our enemies want to keep us trapped. They want us to remain stuck and not live our most fulfilling lives. That's why we must clothe ourselves in God's wisdom which will save us from them all. Men and women both can be immoral. It will be easier to see who is good for us and who is not, the more we align with God's teachings. Pay attention to how someone speaks and acts toward others. It may help us decipher their true character.

February 2nd

"The way of the wicked is like total darkness.
They have no idea what they are stumbling
over."

PROVERBS 4:19

Sin is a slippery slope. When we get caught up in sin, it's like walking in darkness. We can't even see the wrong in what we are doing anymore, tripping over everything and causing devastating consequences to our spiritual health. It's like walking through a dark forest at night. We are left feeling helpless, lost, and confused. That's why we must continuously cling to God, whose light will illuminate our path and clearly show us the way. Sometimes it feels easier to remain in the darkness of sin and the unknown than breaking free into a godly life. Once God's light shines down, trust and follow it fully, don't look back.

February 3rd

"Look straight ahead, and fix your eyes on what lies before you."

PROVERBS 4:25

Sometimes, we look so far ahead in life that we forget to be present in the here and now. When all we see is the end goal, sometimes we will take sinful shortcuts on our road to get there. But it's important to trust God with our future and allow ourselves to be present in the moment, because right now is where we can truly live and impact the world for the better. We can start with one small step, one day at a time. Wake up, make the bed, and brush your teeth. Small actions lead to big results when repeated. The picture of "life" will become clearer if we can embrace living in the moment.

February 4th

"Joyful are those who listen to me (wisdom),
watching for me daily at my gates, waiting for
me outside my home!"

PROVERBS 8:34

True and lasting joy in this life is not to be found in temporary and fleeting pleasures. These things are to be found in God and God alone. His wisdom transforms our lives, allowing us to see the world through His perspective. Then we can live in freedom, resting in His peace, joy, and love. Remember the teaching of instant gratification versus long-term satisfaction. The quick sensation of pleasure will pale in comparison to a hard-fought endeavor. Eating junk food is a great example of this. It will feel good as soon as we eat it. But a few hours later we'll feel greasy and bloated. Eating healthy doesn't give us the same "high" as junk food but will leave us feeling proud of our decision to live a healthy life.

February 5th

"Your kindness will reward you, but your cruelty will destroy you."

PROVERBS 11:17

In every interaction we have in life, we have two options: we can either be kind or cruel. Being kind reflects the love of Jesus to others and builds strong relationships. Being cruel destroys relationships and erodes our character. Which will you choose to live out? Imagine you tried to go one month with only speaking kind words. How do you think your life would improve? If you can picture things around you getting a lot more positive, then maybe it's something to try. Conversely, if we spent one month being cruel, how do you think things would look? Friendships would be strained; relationships would be ruined, and valuable time would be wasted.

February 6th

"Give freely and become more wealthy; be stingy and lose everything."

PROVERBS 11:24

The wisdom of God turns the ways of our world on its head. While the world around us will teach us that being stingy with our money will lead to greater wealth, God tells us that He will bless us abundantly if we use our resources for the betterment of others. Why is this? Because God loves a generous heart, for it reflects His own. For those people, He will pour out His gifts upon them freely. The more we earn, the more we should give. The proverb isn't saying let's be foolish with our money, but rather to be generous and gain much more than what wealth can give us. A full heart, a peaceful mind and a generous spirit are infinitely more valuable.

February 7th

"A troublemaker plants seeds of strife; gossip separates the best of friends."

PROVERBS 16:28

Healthy, thriving, and godly relationships are built on the foundation of kind and encouraging words. The more we speak into the lives of others, the more we build them up and show God's love for them. But gossip, hateful, or cruel words tear a person down and destroy relationships. We must choose to empower those that God has placed in our lives, instead of breaking them down. We will never look back and regret saying kind words to someone else. Try going out of your way to pay someone a compliment today. The smile on their face will be everything.

February 8th

"Fools vent their anger, but the wise quietly hold it back."

PROVERBS 29:11

When facing moments of frustration, we may find a strong urge to vent our anger. This is natural, but we must fight against this tendency. Anger is poison to our souls. It hurts others and broadens the negative feelings within us. We must hold back our anger and always strive for peace instead. We can practice discipline when controlling our reactionary emotions. We can find healthy outlets to release pent up anger like reading, writing, or exercising. Take a step back from the situation and try to see it from a bird's eye view. Whichever is our outlet of choice, we can form a healthy response instead of giving in to negative emotions.

February 9th

"The Lord is more pleased when we do what is right and just than when we offer him sacrifices."

PROVERBS 21:3

God isn't concerned with how much "religious" activity we do. When we become too focused on those types of actions, we start to lose touch of what our faith is truly all about: a personal relationship with God. He wants us to come to Him out of a genuine desire to know Him and be with Him. That's where we truly experience His love. Going to church to practice your faith can be an enriching experience but we all lead busy lives. We shouldn't feel guilt or shame if we aren't able to attend service on a consistent basis. We can continue to practice the way of God in our daily lives and bring Him with us everywhere we go.

February 10ᵗʰ

"No one can comprehend the height of heaven, the depth of the earth, or all that goes on in the king's mind!"

PROVERBS 25:3

As human beings, we have made unbelievable strides in science and technology. We have uncovered a lot of amazing things about the world! But even with all this knowledge, we must remain humble. No matter how much we know, we could never even scratch the surface of what God knows. That's why we must trust in Him and seek His guidance in everything! Picture how much information we consume daily. Sometimes it's overwhelming and overstimulating. Try to spend more time around friends and family and less time on your phone. Screen time keeps us living a virtual life and may take away from living our real life.

February 11th

---

*"Don't brag about tomorrow, since you don't
know what the day will bring."*

PROVERBS 27:1

It's easy to get ahead of ourselves in life. Just because we've planned for or expect something to happen, we can boast confidently about it. We must realize that only God is truly in control, and we don't know what tomorrow will bring. We must trust in His plans above our own and commit to walking where He leads. It's okay for us to be excited about something tomorrow. Maybe it's a raise, a promotion, or a date with a potential partner. But we must be wary about counting chickens before they hatch. If we learn to be content in the moment, any blessings tomorrow will be more of a gift.

February 12th

"Blessed are the generous, because they feed the poor."

PROVERBS 22:9

The sad reality of our world is that not everyone has the same resources and opportunities in our society. There are many people suffering through poverty while many of us live in abundance. We must be willing to give our abundance to ease the suffering of those in need. In doing so, we will be following the example of Jesus. It can be as simple as offering a meal to someone in need. Break bread with someone less fortunate and offer them a helping hand. Being generous feels good. It can breathe new life into us and ignite our spirit from within.

February 13th

"Do you see any truly competent workers? They will serve kings rather than working for ordinary people."

PROVERBS 22:29

Work ethic is important. Our work ethic determines the level of success we will find in life and our ability to support ourselves and our family. God has given us all unique skills to do impactful work in the world. It's crucial that we put forth our full effort toward whatever He has called us to do! No job should be beneath us and no career should be above us. Keep busy with something you enjoy doing and that can contribute positively to others. When we think about others instead of ourselves, we will be even more motivated to show up and work hard each day.

February 14th

"In the blink of an eye wealth disappears, for it will sprout wings and fly away like an eagle."

PROVERBS 23:5

Many people will chase after wealth their entire lives, sacrificing and risking way too much to gain it. Sadly, as time goes on, they've squandered many precious gifts in the pursuit only to find themselves still lacking or to lose all their wealth in the blink of an eye. That's why we should not hold money as an idol in our lives and instead always keep God number one in our hearts. Instead of picturing vast wealth, we can recall three things that we're grateful for and thank God for them.

February 15th

"Don't envy sinners, but always continue to fear the LORD. You will be rewarded for this; your hope will not be disappointed."

PROVERBS 23:17

Sometimes it can be hard not to be envious when we see the worldly things and accomplishments that others possess. They can be very attractive, and we may want them for our own life. But we must continually remember that these are simply fleeting pleasures and that our lasting happiness comes from the rewards we will receive in God's Kingdom when we meet Him in eternity. Instead of constantly comparing ourselves to other people, we should keep track of the progress we make as individuals. We can ask ourselves: is this month better than the previous? Is today better than yesterday? Start small and keep the focus on individual progress.

February 16th

*"The godly may trip seven times, but they will
get up again. But one disaster is enough to
overthrow the wicked."*

PROVERBS 24:16

Even as believers, we will face the struggles in this life. Remember, even Jesus Himself suffered! But faith gives us the strength to push forward, continually getting back up again. Each time, God makes us stronger and pushes us continually toward our eternal destiny in Him. We should not be afraid to make mistakes along the way. God will brighten our darkest days; He will forgive us when we need it most. If we continue to rise after falling, He will reward us with wisdom and knowledge that we lacked prior to sinking. The more times we get up after being knocked down, the easier it will be to bounce back. We can start to view minor setbacks as motivational tools to get further ahead.

February 17th

"Evil people have no future; the light of the wicked will be snuffed out."

God has called us all to live righteous, holy lives. He has made it clear to us through the Scriptures that this is the way to eternal life in His everlasting Kingdom. But those who decide to live sinful lives will not gain eternal life. God has promised to destroy all evil forever when the end times comes. That's why it's crucial that we choose to live by His ways right now: there's no time to waste! Any time spent sinning can be forgiven. One must truly be remorseful and ask God for His forgiveness. If we continue to sin and not feel remorse about it, we run the risk of turning evil. It's okay to make mistakes, but we must be aware of them and seek out God's forgiveness.

50 | R. W. REESE

February 18th

"Let someone else praise you, not your own mouth-a stranger, not your own lips."

PROVERBS 27:2

As a believer, there's no place for pride in our hearts. We must realize that everything we have is a gift from God Himself and not something we have brought about ourselves. That's why we must never boast about ourselves but live in such a way that others praise the way we live and see the benefits of walking with God. It's like the adage of leading by example. Why speak about it when we can just do it instead? If we start to let our godly actions speak for us, they will be much louder than words can ever be.

February 19th

"The heartfelt counsel of a friend is as sweet as perfume and incense."

PROVERBS 27:9

Friendship is a blessing from God, and one we must not take lightly! God has placed others in our life to guide us, walk with us, and encourage us along our journey. Through the fellowship we share with others, we experience God's love. That's why we must commit to seeking out wise and godly friends! Doing so will richly bless our lives. We can aspire to be the person that our friends want to be around. We can counsel them when they seek advice, we can praise them when they need uplifting and be there for them when they call. They will do the same for us.

February 20th

*"As a face is reflected in water, so the heart
reflects the real person."*

PROVERBS 27:19

We must be careful not to wear a disguise in public and
attempt to deceive others into believing we are
something that we aren't. It's important to be genuine and reflect
your true self to others. Our actions will reveal the true nature of
our heart in due time anyway, so trying to hide our real selves is
fruitless. There's a classic saying that we are who we are when no
one else is watching. Do you like the reflection you see?

February 21st

"An evil man is held captive by his own sins; they are ropes that catch and hold him."

PROVERBS 5:22

Never doubt the real and present danger of sin in our lives. Sometimes, it can be easy to brush off what we may consider to be "small" sins. But we must be careful, because even small sins can take hold of our lives and fester in our hearts. We must be proactive against sin in our lives, repenting and giving them over to God daily so that we can live in righteousness. When first finding our faith, small sins may go unnoticed. The more we practice our faith, the more awareness we cast on habits or vices that God would deem destructive. Think about some habits that you'd like to break free from. Pray to God and ask for His help with them.

February 22nd

"She seduced him with her pretty speech, and enticed him with her flattery."

PROVERBS 7:21

Sexual immorality is a real struggle for many people in our world. God has designed sex to be expressed between a man and woman in the confines of marriage, but the world around us doesn't promote it that way. This can cause a lot of tension and confusion in our lives. But we must trust in God's design and attempt to maintain sexual purity throughout our lives. Trust in God that His intent for us was pure. We can ask for his forgiveness when adhering to these wishes is not always possible. For it may seem like an outdated concept, the intention was to limit the ways in which we express intimacy with others. Of course, it won't always be easy to live by, but we can try to honor God's design for us.

February 23rd

*"Wisdom will multiply your days and add years
to your life."*

PROVERBS 9:11

Making wise decisions will benefit our lives in every way, promoting our longevity and helping us to get the most out of life. And who is the ultimate source of wisdom for our lives? God Himself. He speaks to us through His Word, the Holy Bible. When we live by its words, we live a long, blessed life. Instead of making an impulsive decision, we can take a deep breath. We can consult our faith community and most importantly, pray for God's advice. Wise decisions don't happen on an impulse. They are well thought out and take time to make. When stuck on indecision, God will always lead us to the answer. Are we listening?

February 24th

---

*"We have happy memories of the godly, but the
name of a wicked person rots away."*

PROVERBS 10:7

What kind of legacy are you going to leave on the world? The way you live now will determine that. Will people remember you fondly? Or will you have left no impact on the lives of others? These are important questions to consider in the present because they will help motivate us to live righteous, godly lives. Think of how you'd like your friends and family to speak about you when you're not around. Take this image and act like this person to the best of your ability each day.

February 25th

"The fears of the wicked will be fulfilled; the hopes of the godly will be granted."

PROVERBS 10:24

We often bring about our own downfall. Frequently, people's own fears become a reality because of the sinful way they are living their own life. But when we live godly lives and walk in His ways, He will fulfill our hopes and prayers. God listens to the godly and brings about blessed circumstances in their lives! Thoughts are powerful. The more time we spend thinking about something, the more likely we are to bring that thought into our lives. We must learn to relinquish these unnecessary thoughts and fears, instead opting to pray to God. We can fill our hearts and minds with His love.

February 26th

"When the storms of life come, the wicked are whirled away, but the godly have a lasting foundation."

PROVERBS 10:25

There will be storms in life for everyone, they are unavoidable. We live in a fallen and troubled world. But when we walk with God, we have a solid foundation on which to stand and weather the storms. But when we live ungodly lives, the storms will sweep us away. Commit to living a godly life and let the trials ahead serve to strengthen you instead of breaking you! Each time we weather a storm, our foundations will get stronger. The next time a metaphorical storm hits, we'll be able to stand our ground and calmly watch the storm pass by.

.

February 27th

---

*"The mouth of the godly person gives wise advice,
but the tongue that deceives will be cut off."*

PROVERBS 10:31

O ur words are powerful, and we must be careful how we use them. Our words can either build someone up or tear them down. That's why we must use our words to give others wise advice. But we must never attempt to deceive another with our words. That is evil in the eyes of God, and He will punish any who choose to live in that way. Being a trusted source of advice is a high privilege. We must use it wisely to spread His word to those who seek it.

February 28th

"Pride leads to conflict; those who take advice are wise."

PROVERBS 13:10

It's important not to let our pride become so great that we are unable to be coached and refuse to take advice. None of us are perfect and we all have room to grow. That's why we must be willing to take godly advice and make crucial changes in our lives. If not, our pride will only lead to struggles and conflict. We are all self-proclaimed experts in one subject or another. Even with vast knowledge of a particular topic, we should still seek to learn more. We may even learn something from someone, who is less experienced than we are. Don't be above receiving advice. It could lead to the biggest breakthrough of your life.

March 1st

"Hope deferred makes the heart sick, but a dream fulfilled is a tree of life."

PROVERBS 13:12

Hope is a powerful emotion. It helps us to endure challenges in life and look ahead toward a brighter future. But when our hopes don't come to pass, it is hard on our hearts. When we live godly lives, He brings our hopes into fruition. Then, our hearts are full, and we live lives of peace, love, and joy. When starting a new venture, relationship, or job, we must hope that it will be a positive experience. This is more likely to happen if we go into a new situation while living godly lives.

March 2ⁿᵈ

"Wise people think before they act; fools don't- and even brag about their foolishness."

PROVERBS 13:16

Sometimes, it can be hard not to act on our impulses. We have very busy schedules and are always trying to cram things in. It can be easier to act quickly and not take the time to think our decisions through! Maybe it's because we didn't sleep well or are distracted by current events of the world. Still, this is unwise and can lead to disastrous consequences. We must think before we act and measure our decisions against God's standards. A simple way to do this is by taking a step back. Get a good night's rest before making a big decision. We will never regret taking additional time to think something through.

March 3rd

"Why spill the water of your springs in the streets,
having sex with just anyone?"

PROVERBS 5:16

S adly, many people in our world today lead promiscuous lives.
We have largely forgotten the sacredness and holiness of sex
by God's design. Instead, we sin greatly by having sex outside of
its rightful time and place with many partners. Or, by choosing
to view adult content. This is not what pleases God, and it
detracts from a healthy spiritual life. It may not always be
possible to resist such temptations, but if we can develop strong
sexual discipline, we'll experience something even better!

March 4th

"Who can say, 'I have cleansed my heart; I am pure and free from sin?"

PROVERBS 20:9

We live in a fallen world, and no one is perfect. Jesus lived the only sinless life ever lived. We must accept this truth and embrace our need for the salvation of Jesus. When we accept Him as our Savior and walk by His ways, we are clothed in righteousness and are promised eternity in God's everlasting Kingdom. We can learn to live with our mistakes. There will be plenty along the way. But there is knowledge and wisdom to be gained from each misstep. That's why God will always forgive us when we repent, helping to take away our guilt and shame.

March 5th

---

*"Don't trap yourself by making a rash promise to
God and only later counting the cost."*

PROVERBS 20:25

In the heat of a challenging or stressful moment, we can feel a lot of pressure to solve the situation. Sometimes, this will inspire us to make rash promises to God in an effort to petition for His power. But we must be careful what we promise because God takes promises seriously! If we promise anything to God, we must be ready to follow through on whatever it is we have said. If we set realistic expectations for ourselves, we can promise less and deliver more.

March 6th

"The glory of the young is their strength; the gray hair of experience is the splendor of the old."

PROVERBS 20:29

Every season of life has its advantages. Each one is a blessing that we must not take for granted! God has made every era of our lives to be unique. It's up to us to embrace the strengths of our current place in life and live it out to its fullest. When we do, we'll find true contentment in our hearts. We can look back at previous chapters of our lives and see what we are proud of. We can learn from what we are embarrassed by, and we can commit to living each present day in accordance with God no matter what stage of life we're in.

March 7th

*"An employer who hires a fool or bystander is like
an archer who shoots at random."*

PROVERBS 26:10

We all have important work that we do in our lives. It's always helpful to have other skilled people unified in our mission to help us! But we must be wise and cautious about who we work with. If we want to find success with our goals, we must partner with others who are passionate about our work and are up to the task! Do they share our vision? If they don't this can create unwanted drama and stress in our professional lives, which will ultimately spill over into our personal lives too. Instead of randomly picking people to work with, do some research. See if they are aligned with you spiritually.

March 8th

"Better a dry crust eaten in peace than a house filled with feasting-and conflict."

PROVERBS 17:1

Solitude is not always a bad thing. In fact, we all require it at different points in life. Sometimes the best thing for our souls is to spend time alone with God. Even a small circle of deep relationships is better than having many friends that are full of conflict. We must focus on building and strengthening the relationships we have, even if they are few. Would you rather be the gluttonous King or Queen that's mired in scandal, or the family man or woman that leads a simple life? A consistent teaching from the proverbs is that less is more.

March 9th

"Fire tests the purity of silver and gold, but the LORD tests the heart."

PROVERBS 17:3

B lacksmiths use fire to shape, mold, and test the purity of precious metals. In the same way, God uses His power to test the purity of our heart. He sees all and knows all. We must be careful to live righteously, even in private, because nothing is hidden from the eyes of God! If we live an ungodly life in private, but convey that we are holy to the public, how will this benefit us? We must choose to be the same person in private and in public to be truly fulfilled.

March 10th

*"Charm is deceptive, and beauty does not last;
but a woman who fears the LORD will be
greatly praised."*

PROVERBS 31:30

Our society places a lot of focus on people's looks, both women and men. This puts unnecessary pressure on people to feel as if they need to look a certain way or associate with certain people. But we must remember that God has made us all unique and we are all naturally beautiful in our own way. What's much more important than how we look is how we live our lives. That's what God truly cares about.

.

March 11th

---

*"If you repay good with evil, evil will never
leave your house."*

PROVERBS 17:13

We must be diligent in continually fighting against the influence of evil in our lives. When we let it in our heart, even for a moment, it will relentlessly try to grow roots there. If that happens, it will fester and grow until it has taken control of us. Evil is not to be flirted with but fought against at every turn! Imagine an overgrown garden or an uncared-for lawn. It was once a great marvel, but now is a sore to the eyes. Don't let evil overgrow in our own pastures, it will be harder to clean the more it grows wild.

March 12th

"The rich and poor have this in common: The Lord made them both."

PROVERBS 22:2

There are all kinds of people in this world. God made the earth rich in diversity in every way. That's exactly why we can't hold any kind of prejudice in our hearts. God made everyone and loves them all unconditionally. We must do the same, so we can reflect the heart of our Father in heaven. Does it matter if someone has more money than we do? Our goal on this earth is to continue walking down the path God set for us. Be kind to all people along the way. Whether they are educated, rich or poor; we all share the same fate.

March 13th

"The lazy person claims, 'There's a lion out there!
If I go outside, I might be killed."

PROVERBS 22:13

God rewards a solid work ethic. He has given us all unique skills and abilities that He loves to see us utilize for good. Just as a parent is overjoyed at seeing their child succeed through hard work, so too does God find immense joy in seeing us do the same. Don't be lazy and make excuses but work hard for everything you get. Each day is an opportunity to build on the previous. Start your project and refine your craft. Keep the body and mind busy through work ethic and enjoy the fulfillment that comes with it.

March 14th

"My child, eat honey, for it is good, and the honeycomb is sweet to the taste."

PROVERBS 24:13

While hard work and righteous living is important, God wants us to enjoy the pleasures of life as well. God has created a beautiful diversity of foods, landscapes, and pursuits for us to enjoy in life. He desires for us to enjoy our lives and experience the world He created us to live in. Take time to nourish properly, eat good foods, drink clean water and rest well. Hard work will be rewarded. So too will taking care of your body, mind, and spirit.

March 15th

"An honest answer is like a kiss of friendship."

PROVERBS 24:26

Have you heard the saying, "honesty is the best policy?" It's used frequently, but it's true. God commands us to be honest in everything, even when it's hard. Honesty builds unbreakable relationships with others and gives us a good reputation. Honesty will serve you greatly in life and is a virtue worth striving for in every way. Even if it's a hard truth to tell, speak it. People will respect you more for always being honest, even if the truth is harder to hear initially.

March 16th

"*Do your planning and prepare your fields
before building your house.*"

PROVERBS 26:27

There cannot be enough said about the importance of planning and preparation. When we rush into something blindly, it rarely goes as smoothly as we hope. Chance isn't enough. Anything worth doing is also worth putting the time and effort into preparing for. We can create our own life's vision by planning for our future. Tend to the smaller things first, and then progress onto bigger concerns. Start each day by making the bed, the good habits will stack up, and soon you'll have the home you desire.

March 17th

---

*"The godly care for their animals, but the wicked
are cruel."*

PROVERBS 12:10

God created the world and everything in it. That includes
the rich diversity of the animal kingdom! Every animal,
both big and small, was created from the mind of God. That
means they deserve our love, care, and respect. Those who love
God will care for His creations and respect His divinely inspired
design. Whether it's a house dog or cat, big livestock at a farm,
or fish in the ocean, each serves a vital role in our ecosystem. God
gave each animal a purpose that is equal to our own. Treat them
with respect, thank them for their lives and treat them like you
would treat another human being.

March 18th

*"Guard your heart above all else, for it
determines the course of your life."*

PROVERBS 4:23

This verse contains one of the greatest pieces of wisdom in the Bible. The heart is the root of our emotions, which largely guides our actions. It's of utmost importance that we engage in things that promote the wellness of our emotional stability. When our heart is full of joy and at peace, the rest of our life will be blessed. If we must make a big life decision, it's vital that our heart be in good spirits to guide our decision. If it's filled with love, we'll be able to make much holier decisions, than if it's filled with hate.

March 19th

"Mark out a straight path for your feet; stay on the safe path."

PROVERBS 4:26

When we build a strong, personal relationship with God, He clears a path for us in life. All we must do is follow Him and He will guide our way. There will be many things trying to pull us off that path, but we must be diligent in following it throughout our life. There have never been more meaningless distractions than in our modern day with social media, news, and endless online content. We will each occasionally wander from our path, but with God's plan in mind, we will keep returning to our intended destination.

March 20th

"Gentle words are a tree of life; a deceitful
tongue crushes the spirit."

PROVERBS 15:4

The words we speak are crucial. We carry more power in our words than we could ever know. When we speak kind, gentle words, we build others up. But when we lie, deceive, and speak ill of others, our words are like poison to those we speak to. Think long and hard before you speak and only say things which are beneficial to others. It could even start with our thoughts. If we aren't thinking good things, we likely aren't saying good things. Begin with positive self-talk, and it will be much easier to vocalize kind words.

March 21st

"She is clothed with strength and dignity, and
she laughs without fear of the future."

PROVERBS 31:25

Proverbs 31 describes the virtuous traits of a godly woman, but there is wisdom that we can all apply to our daily lives. We must work toward growing in strength and dignity. When we place our trust in God, we gain strength from His power and joy from our identity as His children. These traits help us look boldly toward the future without fear or worry. It can be especially difficult in societies where religion is mocked. But we must keep placing our faith in God and letting His wisdom guide us.

March 22nd

"People ruin their lives by their own foolishness and then are angry at the LORD."

PROVERBS 19:3

Have you noticed how quick a lot of people are to blame God for the circumstances of their life? But when we are honest with ourselves and look at the path that led us to where we are, we can be the authors of our own downfall. We must take responsibility for our actions and follow the path that God has paved for us. There are many ways we can commit self-destructing behaviors. Recognize these habits. Rid the guilt and shame that they bring. Learn from them and accept that we have control over our lives. We have the power to seek God and ask for his guidance.

March 23rd

"Haughty eyes, a proud heart, and evil actions are all sin."

PROVERBS 21:4

When we think of sin, we often think of doing bad things. Yes, evil actions are sins, but so are many other things. Corrupt or twisted thoughts, pride in our hearts, and lying are all other examples of sin. We must guard our hearts against them all! It's impossible to think only positive thoughts. We all have moments of weakness or a lack of self-control. But the more we practice God's intention for us, the more positive our thoughts will naturally become. This will lead to a healthier lifestyle and more meaningful relationships.

March 24ᵗʰ

"Wealth created by a lying tongue is a vanishing mist and a deadly trap."

PROVERBS 21:6

We must work honestly for anything that we gain in life. If we become wealthy or prosperous in any way, it only means something if we have gone about it by honest and just means. If we have lied or deceived to get where we are in life, our prosperity and riches will mean nothing and vanish as quickly as we gained them in the first place. There is nothing wrong with financial freedom, it should be aspired to by all. But, if it comes at the cost of deceiving other people, too much karmic debt will be incurred. Stick to work that can be beneficial to others, and we can be wealthy in many ways.

March 25th

*"Those who shut their ears to the cries of the poor
will be ignored in their own time of need."*

PROVERBS 21:13

God has called us to live our lives in service to others, just as
Jesus did. When we do, we are counted among God's
children and embark on a quest to become more like Jesus.
When we cut ourselves off from a relationship with God by
ignoring His commands, we also cast aside His favor and help in
times of need. We will all face unique series of challenges
throughout life. It could be financial hardship, loss of a loved
one, or business ventures that aren't prosperous. We never know
when these things may come up. Extend a helping hand to those
in need and they'll do the same for you.

March 26th

*"Some who are poor pretend to be rich; others
who are rich pretend to be poor."*

PROVERBS 13:7

It's hard to tell someone's life circumstances just by looking at them. Some in poverty will often try to hide it for fear of feeling shame or rejection. Then there are wealthy people who will live simply and keep their riches private. It's just another reminder to never judge a book by its cover. We will never truly know what someone else is going through. Nor do we need to. If we live with God's intentions in mind, we can treat everyone in our lives as equal beings.

March 27th

*"An unreliable messenger stumbles into trouble,
but a reliable messenger brings healing."*

PROVERBS 13:17

Being reliable is a virtuous trait we should all strive for. When we're reliable, we earn people's trust. We build relationships that lead us to a beautiful and prosperous life. Fickleness erodes at the foundation of relationships, but reliability brings healing. Strive to be there consistently for someone else. Show up with a positive attitude, an open mind, and a kind word. The more reliable we are, the greater chance we have at making a positive impact for someone else.

March 28th

"The LORD's light penetrates the human spirit,
exposing every hidden motive."

PROVERBS 20:27

It's not just about what we do, but the motives behind what we are doing. Sometimes, the "why" can be just as important, or even more important, than the "what." Anything we do that's not done out of godly love is empty, shallow, and ultimately without purpose. We must devote every aspect of our lives to the building up of God's Kingdom! God will see through impure intentions. We should establish our "why" with God in mind and attempt our best to remain devoted to His teachings throughout our journey.

March 29th

"Justice is a joy to the godly, but it terrifies evildoers."

PROVERBS 21:15

Evil is prevalent in our world. When evil actions are committed against people, it breaks God's heart. He loves everyone and hates to see people hurting. Evil is the opposite of everything God is! That's why the righteous love justice. Evil deserves to be conquered. But those who practice it are terrified of justice, knowing their actions will come back to haunt them. Those who perform evil acts will carry around guilt and shame. It might not come back to haunt them right away, but eventually it will catch up with them.

March 30th

"Choose a good reputation over great riches;
being held in high esteem is better than silver or
gold."

PROVERBS 22:1

A good reputation brings with it thriving relationships, great opportunities in life, and honor for you and your family. These are all things to strive for and work toward. But money without these things is fleeting, pointless, and meaningless. We must choose to focus on how we live and not how wealthy we are. The more we aspire to live with the right intentions, the greater the likelihood that we'll find wealth in one form or another.

March 31st

*"Direct your children onto the right path, and
when they are older, they will not leave it."*

PROVERBS 22:6

Teaching our children about faith and godly character is crucial to their development. When we teach them at an early age, our instruction will stick with them as they get older. But we must be sure to practice what we teach as well. They will respond to what we do more than what we say! Often, we want to correct or change a behavior by speaking. Instead, we can implement the change through our actions and lead by setting strong examples.

April 1st

"Do you like honey? Don't eat too much, or it will make you sick!

PROVERBS 25:16

While it's probably not something you think about every day, gluttony is a real threat and sin in our lives. In our modern, fast-paced world, it's easy to overeat and justify our actions. But it will eventually catch up to us and could have devastating effects on our health! Too much consumption of just about anything will often have the opposite effect and could lead to problems if undisciplined. A good life philosophy to live by is to produce more and consume less.

April 2nd

*"If your enemies are hungry, give them food to
eat. If they are thirsty, give them water to drink."*

PROVERBS 25:21

Revenge is never a good idea. It bears no fruit and doesn't
remove the original injustice committed. You can't go back
in time and erase what happened. The best thing we can do is
practice forgiveness and choose to extend love to those who hurt
us in hopes that healing can be found all-around. Life is too short
to try and "get back" at someone else. We can simply care for
those who have wronged us like friends and family. Lend them a
kind word and don't react to their negativity. We can have a
much greater impact if we choose to act in a positive manner
rather than stew in negativity.

April 3rd

"Alcohol is for the dying, and wine for those in bitter distress."

PROVERBS 31:6

In our current world, alcohol has gained a reputation for being a social activity. It is celebrated as fun, and friends will urge each other to join in. Sadly, this leads many down a devastating path. Alcohol is not something to joke about or abuse as a social activity for the sake of pleasing our friends. We must learn to use it responsibly. There is nothing wrong with a glass of wine here and there or toasting with champagne on a holiday. But habits are much easier to form than to break. We should use caution when dealing with alcohol and ask ourselves if it's masking anything else in our lives.

April 4th

---

*"The LORD corrects those He loves, just as a
father corrects a child in whom he delights."*

PROVERBS 3:12

God wants the best for us in life. He desires nothing more
than to see us grow into happy, healthy people with love,
joy, and peace in our hearts. Just as a child needs direction to
grow, so too do we need direction as we grow in spiritual
maturity. We must accept God's correction and embrace that it's
leading us to being more complete, godly people. Sometimes the
best mentorship is provided in the form of correcting. Not in a
controlling way, but in a teaching way when wanting to see
others blossom and grow.

April 5th

"Wisdom is a tree of life to those who embrace her; happy are those who hold her tightly."

PROVERBS 3:18

Wisdom is the greatest gift we could ever receive in life. Wisdom gives to us continuously and builds deep and godly character within us. When we cling to wisdom, we commit ourselves to continued spiritual growth. We make great decisions all through our lives and prosper because of it. Wisdom isn't learned overnight. It's not suddenly surrounding us in life. It comes through the curiosity to learn, the ability to admit wrongdoings, and the capacity to ask for forgiveness.

April 6th

---

*"The LORD is your security. He will keep your
foot from being caught in a trap."*

PROVERBS 3:26

When we walk through life alongside God, He protects us. His power is beyond anything we could ever know or imagine, and He withholds nothing in His protection of us. The devil is real and wishes to pull us off our God-given path. But when we cling to God, we can trust that He will shield us from all evil. There is evil lurking all around us in our modern-day world. Distractions will present themselves to us daily. Temptations will be plentiful. We can acknowledge that these evils exist and latch on closer to God.

April 7th

"Don't pick a fight without reason, when no one has done you harm."

PROVERBS 3:30

You've probably known someone in your life who seems to seek out conflict. While sad, some people thrive on it. Conflict hurts others and destroys relationships. It's not healthy for us physically, emotionally, or spiritually to live that way. We must honor and cherish every relationship as a gift from God. There will be highs and lows in all relationships. It doesn't mean we should ride the rollercoaster. We are capable of remaining kind and neutral in all situations. We can use the love in our hearts from God to avoid unnecessary confrontations.

April 8th

"All who fear the LORD will hate evil."

PROVERBS 8:13

Anything evil is the opposite of what God is. God hates evil because it goes against His perfect design for us and the world. He created us to live in love, peace, and joy but evil attempts to take that all away. We must never tolerate or embrace it. If we let it, evil will consume us. Though we should not fear it. The only thing we should be fearful of is God. We should be in awe of his creations and honor him in the highest light.

April 9th

"The LORD formed me from the beginning,
before He created anything else."

PROVERBS 8:22

This proverb is spoken from wisdom's point of view. God created wisdom before setting the foundations of the world, meaning that everything was built upon wisdom. That's why godly wisdom is essential for our lives. Our entire world, and even our very own design, were patterned after it. If we are to truly understand the world and our place in it, we must embrace God's wisdom. Place trust in knowing everything He created was for a purpose. It may not be clear to us yet, but the more we practice faith, the more clarity we can gain.

April 10th

"Fear of the LORD is the foundation of wisdom. Knowledge of the Holy One results in good judgment."

PROVERBS 9:10

Having good judgment is vital to the success of our lives. Good judgment makes for good decisions, and good decisions lead to innumerable benefits. We must have love, knowledge, and reverence for God to find good judgment in life. God and His wisdom will never lead us astray. If we consistently practice good judgment, our lives will improve drastically. Make one better decision each day and watch your life transform.

April 11th

"The king's fury is like a lion's roar; to rouse his anger is to risk your life."

PROVERBS 20:2

While we know that God is loving and cherishes us all as the beautiful individuals He's created us to be, we must also keep a healthy fear and reverence of Him in our hearts. We should strive to please Him and not anger Him. His power is unmatchable, and He cannot stand evil. If we commit evil without repentance, we put ourselves in danger of His almighty power. Try your best to live in His good graces. And if you ever stray from your moral standards, ask Him to forgive you.

April 12th

*"Trust in your money and down you go! But the
godly flourish like leaves in spring."*

PROVERBS 11:28

M any people place their trust in money and worldly riches.
They believe that money will give them security and joy.
But those things are fleeting when based upon wealth. Only God
can give true and lasting security and joy. It's best that we place
the fullness of our faith in Him! There are few certainties in life.
Obtaining and keeping wealth is not one of them. While many
of us may wish for worldly riches, we must not lose sight of all
the blessings we currently have. Praise God and be thankful for
all He's blessed you with.

April 13th

"Wrongdoers eagerly listen to gossip; liars pay close attention to slander."

PROVERBS 17:4

In our society today, gossip is encouraged and sometimes celebrated. In certain circles, being prone to gossip can make you a lot of friends! But those are NOT the kind of relationships we want to build in our lives. We want to focus our time and energy on godly relationships that will build us up in our faith. To find those kinds of relationships, we must stay far away from gossip. Speak about others with kindness. We should only say things in private that other people would be comfortable hearing if they were in the room with us. If we have the urge to gossip about others, it may be because our own personal lives are lacking something.

April 14th

---

*"To learn, you must love discipline; it is stupid
to hate correction."*

PROVERBS 12:1

For many of us, it is natural for us to get defensive when being corrected. But it's crucial that we change our perception of what it means to be corrected. It is not meant to shame us or bring us down, but rather to help us to grow and excel in godliness. When we think of it that way, we'll welcome and encourage corrections! Our lives will only be better for it. We must learn to take ourselves less seriously. Be able to laugh at oneself when we are corrected, for we will learn much more from that than approaching a similar situation with anger.

April 15th

"Worry weighs a person down; an encouraging word cheers a person up."

PROVERBS 12:25

Worry and anxiety weigh heavily upon human hearts. Sadly, we live in a world where these feelings fester and grow in the hearts of many. We must recognize this and speak joy and peace into the lives of others. Commit to speaking only encouraging words to others that will help to ease the burden on their hearts. We can take hold of our anxiety by returning to our roots. Seek nature and maintain a healthy relationship with God. Let go of your worries when able and lift the people around you so they can do the same for you.

April 16th

"Lazy people don't even cook the game they catch, but the diligent make use of everything they find."

PROVERBS 12:27

Imagine fishing or hunting and not even preparing and eating the animals you have killed. What a waste! But sadly, this is exactly what being lazy is like. We have been given skills and resources to do incredible things in this life. When we take those things for granted and don't use them, we dishonor God. If ever in those situations, thank the animals for the nutrition they provide and share a meal with a loved one. God gave us incredible resources on this earth that we should be respectful of.

April 17th

"The tongue of the wise makes knowledge appealing, but the mouth of a fool belches out foolishness."

PROVERBS 15:2

When we devote ourselves to godly knowledge, we inspire others to seek out such godly knowledge as well. But when we are foolish, we destroy our own reputation and don't inspire others toward anything. Choose how you live your life carefully. You can impact the lives of others and have a great responsibility in doing so! Think about if you just impacted one person positively each week. And then if that person followed in your teachings and went on to do the same. The world would be a much better place.

April 18th

"The LORD detests the sacrifice of the wicked,
but He delights in the prayers of the upright."

PROVERBS 15:8

If we are living lives of sin and wickedness, no number of religious sacrifices or actions will mean anything. We can't make the mistake of thinking we can cover up unrepented sin with religious sacrifices. The way we find forgiveness for our sin is to repent and strive toward a different life through the guidance of God. If we feel genuine remorse and want to change our actions, God will understand and forgive us. But we must not take that for granted. Remain under high moral conduct and He'll be delighted by your prayers.

April 19th

"A glad heart makes a happy face; a broken heart crushes the spirit."

PROVERBS 15:13

While it's easy to have a pessimistic attitude in the face of the struggles we have in life, it's crucial that we work toward godly joy in our lives. We can choose to be happy despite our circumstances, and we can find joy in God. Joy is contagious and spreads to others in our lives. But despair only crushes us and those we love. Think of how much more pleasant a smiling face is compared with a frowning one. Happiness stems from within our heart. Fulfill that and our faces will glow.

April 20th

"A bowl of vegetables with someone you love is better than steak with someone you hate."

PROVERBS 15:17

Mealtime is a sacred moment where we forge inseparable bonds with others. It is an intimate time where we let our guard down and join in a genuine relationship. It's important that we treat mealtime with respect and care, sharing it with those that bring love, joy, and peace to our lives. The company you keep during mealtime is much more important than the food on your plate! It's less about the quality of food, the restaurant name, or the menu selection. The people sitting around you at the table and the conversation you'll share is far greater.

April 21st

"Foolishness brings joy to those with no sense; a sensible person stays on the right path."

PROVERBS 15:21

Sometimes we see people that are content with living their lives in sin. This can be confusing because we want the happiness that we see in them. Not to mention, living a godly life is a lot more difficult. But rest assured that sin will catch up with them and keep them from salvation. We are right to walk the righteous path in God. Some days we feel confused or doubt creeps in about the path we're on. That's normal. Choosing the right path takes additional time, effort, and patience. We will be rewarded for it.

April 22nd

"Greed brings grief to the whole family, but those who hate bribes will live."

PROVERBS 15:27

Greed is a cancer in our hearts, growing and growing until we can no longer control it. Sadly, it affects not only us, but those we love as well. We must responsibly live our lives because the bad choices we make have a ripple effect and hurt the ones we love. God has put them in our life as a blessing and we must honor it by taking care of them. Imagine if we chose to enjoy our journey through life, rather than continually daydreaming about having more. Being content with what we have does not equal complacency.

April 23rd

*"The LORD is far from the wicked, but He
hears the prayers of the righteous."*

PROVERBS 15:29

Faith is all about having a personal relationship with God. When we live sinful lives, we will not experience God's presence. But when we walk down the path He has paved before us, He is close to us, gladly walking with us through every experience. Cling to righteousness and God will be nearby! Know that he's always near us and never far from us when we need him. Though we risk his closeness when we continue to live in sin. If we stay on His chosen path for us, He will reward us in many ways.

April 24th

---

*"Fear of the LORD teaches wisdom; humility
precedes honor."*

PROVERBS 15:33

When we believe in God, we believe in His mighty power
and authority. We should fear God, not because we
believe He dislikes us, but because we know that He loves us and
wants us to stay on the path He has shown us. We should desire
to please Him in all we do and see His mighty power work for
us and not against us. Our hearts should hunger to be in good
standing with God! When we are in flow with God, it's like
sailing with full wind behind us.

April 25th

"Unfriendly people care only about themselves;
they lash out at common sense."

PROVERBS 18:1

How we treat others is important. When we are friendly, we build great relationships that benefit our lives, and we build up others as well. But when we are unfriendly, we cultivate selfishness in our hearts and destroy the blessed relationships we have. Think about some unfriendly people you know in your life. Do you think they are genuinely mean people, or that something in their life may not be going right? Though it's difficult, we can choose to extend kindness to them too without expecting anything in return. This could have a profound impact on them.

April 26th

"Fools have no interest in understanding; they only want to air their own opinions."

PROVERBS 18:2

Have you ever encountered someone who doesn't seem to listen and only wants to speak their own mind? That is exactly the kind of person this verse speaks to. If we want to experience thriving and happy relationships with others, we must have empathy, genuinely listening to the thoughts and needs of others. Sometimes fools teach us the biggest lessons. Looking at someone that you aspire not to be is just as powerful as having a role model. Be the person that speaks less and listens more.

April 27th

"The rich think of their wealth as a strong defense; they imagine it to be a high wall of safety."

PROVERBS 18:11

People put way too much faith in worldly wealth. They believe that if they can simply make enough money, that everything else will fall into place. But this way of living is a deception. True security and safety come from God and God alone. We can lose our wealth in a moment, but God will be by our side forever. Financial freedom can bring worldly experiences but be conscious of how quickly it can all disappear. God will be there for us no matter what our financial situations look like.

April 28th

"The first to speak in court sound right-until the cross examination begins."

PROVERBS 18:17

We must carefully consider the words and opinions of others. Those who are good at speaking can argue for anything and make it sound true. But when we think through something that's not right, it's true nature will be revealed. Weigh everything against the standard of God's word and you will never be led astray. We typically only hear one side of an argument at first and could be quick to form judgments based on that. We must practice patience and reserve judgment until we hear the full story.

April 29th

"There are 'friends' who destroy each other, but a real friend sticks closer than a brother."

True friendship is revealed through our actions, not only by our words. When we truly love and care for another person, we are there for them when they are in need. We don't tear that person down or make them feel lesser-than. Friendships like this can be even closer than relationships with our own family! Friendships can come and go in life but think of the ones that have stood the test of time. These friendships are sacred. Sometimes people just want to leech off us and these "friends" will be revealed over time.

THE DAILY PROVERBS | 121

April 30th

"The guilty walk a crooked path; the innocent travel a straight road."

PROVERBS 21:8

When we are living sinful lives, we are always taking shortcuts and looking for ways to deviate off the path we know is right. But when we are living righteously, we simply continue to walk the path ahead of us. We make things more complicated than they need to be. God has placed the correct path before us, all we must do is walk it! Sometimes this path will be boring. Sometimes we'll glance over to the crooked path and think the ups and downs of it look more fun. That won't be the case. The slow and steady path set before us from God is the only road worth traveling.

May 1st

"The person who strays from common sense will end up in the company of the dead."

PROVERBS 21:16

There's a lot to be said for common sense. We all have an instinctual understanding of what is right and how we should live. But when our desires consume us, we try to justify and explain our sinful habits so we can live in a way that's more pleasurable. But this will only lead to our downfall! Constantly seeking pleasure will deviate us off our intended path and lead us into a life full of sin. The right path may seem harder but will be much more rewarding in the long run.

May 2nd

"No human wisdom or understanding or plan can stand against the LORD."

PROVERBS 21:30

This is a proverb we'd be wise to commit to memory. We must know our place, realizing that we are people and God is God! He is perfect, all-powerful, and holds all authority over heaven and earth. Nothing we do in opposition to Him will bear any fruit in our lives. We must devote ourselves to Him in every way. It's the same principle as karmic debt. The more we do right, the more success we have. The more we do wrong, the more negative results we should expect.

May 3rd

"The wicked run away when no one is chasing them, but the godly are as bold as lions."

PROVERBS 28:1

When we live sinful lives, deep in our hearts we know we are doing wrong. We try to run from our misdeeds and cover up our sins. But when we live righteous lives in the eyes of God, we don't have to worry about doing such things. We can stand tall and firm on our strength in God, valiantly facing whatever life may bring. The wicked will always fear their own shadow. The godly have nothing to fear except God himself.

May 4th

"God detests the prayers of a person who ignores the law."

PROVERBS 28:9

We can't think that praying will cover up our sins if we ignore the way God has called us to live. We must think about our motives and intentions because they are important. If we are praying to comfort ourselves or to get rid of our guilt, it is not enough! We must be committed to making actual changes in our lives for prayer to bear fruit. Even if we make small mistakes while attempting to change for the better, it's okay! If our intention is pure and we are committed to getting better, God will have patience for us.

May 5th

"A wicked ruler is as dangerous to the poor as a roaring lion or an attacking bear."

PROVERBS 28:15

When we find ourselves in positions of leadership, we must take the responsibility seriously. The people we are serving through our leadership depend on us and we have great influence over their lives. That's why we must reflect God's loving and merciful nature toward them. In doing so, we will show them the love of Christ. Being a positive leader can have a great impact on many people. Conversely, being a phony ruler will cause many to question the true intentions of those in power. If ever put in a position of leadership, treat it seriously. Learn from those who misled many unsuspecting people.

May 6th

---

*"The blameless will be rescued from harm, but
the crooked will be suddenly destroyed."*

PROVERBS 28:18

When we walk in close relationship with God, His protection covers us. He loves us as His beloved children and will not let us come to harm. But when we choose to live far from God, we are no longer covered by His protection. We must choose to walk with God through every season of our lives. Walking without guilt and shame will help us lead fulfilling lives. When we carry too much burden on our backs, it will take away from enjoying life for what it is.

May 7th

"Showing partiality is never good, yet some will do wrong for a mere piece of bread."

PROVERBS 28:21

We must be fair and honest with everyone. Showing partiality to some and making things harder for others is unfair. We must never cut corners because it will only hurt us in the long run. The momentary reward of cutting that corner is fleeting, but the eternal reward of doing the right thing is everlasting! The longer, more untraveled road can lead to much greater things than taking the quick shortcut to a known destination.

May 8th

"Greed causes fighting; trusting the LORD leads to prosperity."

PROVERBS 28:25

When we want more than we have, greed is prevailing in our hearts. We must find contentment in what we have and never place worldly status or possessions above other people. We must trust in God to provide for our needs and never let greed come between us and the relationships God has placed within our lives. Our relationships with God, friends and family are significantly more important in life than material possessions. We all share the same fate, who are we trying to impress?

May 9th

"When the wicked take charge, people go into hiding. When the wicked meet disaster, the godly flourish."

PROVERBS 28:28

Throughout history, we see that wicked rulers have prospered and hurt the people they were supposed to serve. This has happened all over the world. Thankfully, the reverse has also been true. When these rulers lose power, the godly flourish once again. We must ensure that we do everything we can to put godly rulers in charge of our government because this is still an issue we face today! There has never been more of a greater divide between people among beliefs than there is in the modern day. We can change this by practicing respecting other opinions even if it is challenging at first.

May 10th

"Avoiding a fight is a mark of honor; only fools insist on quarreling."

PROVERBS 20:3

There is never a point to senseless arguing and fighting with others. All it leads to is broken relationships and a degradation of character. We must strive for peace in every situation, not thinking so highly of our own opinion that we are willing to destroy relationships and lessen our character to "win" the argument. Let your heart be set upon God's peace! Trust your gut. And trust God's plan for you. But don't compromise relationships with others over deep-rooted stubbornness.

May 11th

---

*"Don't say, 'I will get even for this wrong.' Wait
for the LORD to handle the matter."*

PROVERBS 20:22

Revenge doesn't solve anything. It may make you feel better for a moment, but it only causes more pain on top of the anguish you've already experienced. Not only that, but it makes you do ungodly things. Revenge does not line up with the way we've been called to live. When we seek revenge, we go against God's will for our lives. There is nothing to be vengeful over. Feeling sorry for those that have wronged us is infinitely more influential.

May 12th

*"Like a fluttering sparrow or a darting swallow,
an undeserved curse will not land on its intended
victim."*

PROVERBS 26:2

Wishing bad things upon another person is hateful and evil. God has called us to be loving and caring toward everyone. God will protect those close to Him, so our curses will not even cause the hurt that we want them to. It's best that we live by the will of God instead, practicing forgiveness and love in all situations. It's difficult to forgive those who have wronged us. But practicing this challenging behavior will help us to experience growth in our lives. The more we grow, the more capable of loving we become.

May 13th

"Honoring a fool is as foolish as tying a stone to a slingshot."

PROVERBS 26:8

Tying a stone to a slingshot kind of defeats the purpose, doesn't it? A slingshot is designed to make a stone fly! It's the same way when we honor and celebrate the foolish actions of others: it's pointless. Not only that, but it also encourages their sinful behavior which will not help bring them back into a relationship with God.

May 14th

"There is more hope for fools than for people who think they are wise."

PROVERBS 26:12

People who struggle in their foolish behavior but genuinely want to do better can find forgiveness in God. But those who are stubborn in their ways and think they have it all figured out will never come to repentance until they change that mindset. To receive the salvation of Christ, we must accept that we are sinners with limited human knowledge that need the power of God in our lives. When one walks by an ocean, a big forest, or tall mountains, they are quickly humbled. Carry this experience with you in daily life. Choose to be humble and consistently strive to learn more.

May 15th

*"Wise words will win you a good meal, but
treacherous people have an appetite for violence."*

PROVERBS 13:2

We must hunger for wisdom and godly discernment in the
Lord above all. When sin enters our hearts, we will find
ourselves craving sinful things. When this happens, we must
fight against it, rooting out our sinful desires and replacing them
with godly ones instead. Then we will be able to speak wise
words into the lives of others and feast on the infinite wisdom of
God. It starts with baby steps. Replace one bad habit with a good
one. Chip away at it until that bad habit whittles down to its
core.

May 16th

---

*"If you set a trap for others, you will get caught
in it yourself."*

PROVERBS 26:27

Evil does not recognize a master. Just because you are the one who has plotted evil against someone else doesn't mean that that evil won't be around and catch you instead. In fact, it often will! The sins we commit have a way of catching up with us and wreaking havoc in our lives. Choose to live a godly life instead. Trust in God and trust His plan for you. If we live in a constant state of paranoia, we will be consumed by it and unable to fully enjoy the beautiful life that God has created for us.

May 17th

"The LORD will not let the godly go hungry,
but He refuses to satisfy the craving of the
wicked."

PROVERBS 10:3

We spend so much of our time and energy chasing wealth in this life, thinking that if we have enough money, we will be able to provide for all our wants and needs. What we fail to realize is that God is the true provider of everything in life. Instead of turning toward money, we must place our faith in Him. He will never lead us astray and He will fulfill all of our needs. The more possessions we crave, the bigger the void will become within us. Think of someone you know, who has everything they could possibly want. How does their life really look?

May 18th

"The earnings of the godly enhance their lives,
but evil people squander their money on sin."

PROVERBS 10:16-17

When we live righteously, we are wise with our money. We don't waste it on sinful or fleeting pleasures. God has given us money as a stewardship in which to do good things for His Kingdom with. When we invest our money in churches and ministries that are doing God's work, we are good stewards of the resources that God has entrusted us with. If it's not a church or ministry you want to put your money in, think about your children or family that needs it. Aspire to give children the life that you wanted for yourself.

May 19th

"Lazy people are soon poor; hard workers get rich."

PROVERBS 10:4

This proverb is as simple as they come: hard work pays off! God blesses our hard work with wealth. But when we are lazy, we are not rewarded. We all get opportunities in life, and we must ensure that we take advantage of those breaks when they arise. God will recognize the effort we are putting in and honor our hard work. If you're ever struck with a great idea, don't let it go to waste. Turn your vision into a reality and thank God for your creativity to see it through. If we let opportunities pass us by, we'll always look back and wonder "what if?"

May 20th

"Upright citizens are good for a city and make it prosper, but the talk of the wicked tears it apart."

PROVERBS 11:11

A community is only as strong as the people who are in it. When a community is filled with godly people, it flourishes. But the lies, deceit, hate, and other sinful actions of the wicked can quickly tear other people apart. Choose to be an upright citizen so that your community can flourish and experience what being a child of God is all about! Be the person you want others to look up to in your community. Think of how much further you could go with the support of your team or community, than you could by yourself.

May 21st

"The LORD detests people with crooked hearts,
but He delights in those with integrity."

PROVERBS 11:20

God's standards and definition of success are much different than those of the world. What true success looks like in the eyes of the Lord is moral integrity and upright character. Those should be our greatest goals in this life. When we can achieve that, we will please God and He will shine his light on us. Remember, we are who we are when no one is watching. Are you proud of the person you are when you're by yourself? Be true to God and honor yourself even when no one else is around.

May 22nd

"The seeds of good deeds become a tree of life; a wise person wins friends."

PROVERBS 11:30

Doing good and righteous deeds in this life is like planting a tree. The more we water and care for it, the more it will grow and bring good fruit into the world. We will be close to God, have amazing friends, and prosper in everything we do. If we want to live a blessed life, we must focus on living in a way that pleases God. The better deeds we do, the better karma we will have. The better our relationship with God will be and the healthier relationships we will attract into our lives.

May 23rd

"The godly hate lies; the wicked cause shame and disgrace."

PROVERBS 13:5

Lying is almost commonplace in our world, and it's a tragedy. God is the author of truth and anything that is a lie is in direct opposition to Him. That's why we must hate lies and cling to the truth. Lies will lead us to ruin but the truth will lead us straight into the arms of God for all eternity. Lies can ruin friendships, relationships, and business opportunities. Truth builds a solid foundation for any venture. Why compromise something good over a few untrue words?

May 24th

"Deceit fills hearts that are plotting evil; joy fills hearts that are planning peace!"

PROVERBS 12:20

Everything we say and do should be targeted toward promoting peace and love to everyone around us. If we plan and commit selfish, hurtful actions, deceit will fill our hearts and come to consume us. Sin only gives rise to more sin, and before we know it, it's too late to turn back. That's why we must embrace the joy that comes from living a life of godly peace! Speak truthfully, love fully, and keep devoting yourself to God. If we strive to walk in these ways each day, our hearts will be filled with joy, and we'll be able to appreciate the little things in life.

May 25th

"It is pleasant to see dreams come true, but fools refuse to turn from evil to attain them."

PROVERBS 13:19

We all have dreams in life, but sadly we frequently don't do what's necessary to turn them into reality. Instead, we turn to sinful shortcuts and then blame God when things don't go our way. What we must realize is that if we walk a godly path and practice patience, God will bring us the desires of our hearts! Try to accomplish your dreams with the intention of uplifting others along the way. The better we do, the more fruitful our ventures will be. Seek to help those around you and you'll have the energy needed to reach your goals.

May 26th

"Laughter can conceal a heavy heart, but when the laughter ends, the grief remains."

PROVERBS 14:13

When we are hurting, it can be our natural response to try and hide it. We want to put on a brave face for people and give the impression that we are okay. But it's important that we confront the grief that's in our hearts. When we do, God will bring us to healing. We can trust godly friends in our life to help us through this journey. Every emotion that we have should be acknowledged. It's good to be mindful of the ups and the downs equally in life and try to remain somewhere in between, rather than riding a constant emotional rollercoaster.

May 27th

"If you plan to do evil, you will be lost; if you plan to do good, you will receive unfailing love and faithfulness."

PROVERBS 14:22

When we live sinful lives, we become lost. Why? Because we've strayed off the clear path God has set before us. Yet when we do good and live righteously, we follow a road that leads us to the unfailing love and faithfulness of God, our Creator. His love is unlike any we have ever known before, and it will keep us safe and secure for eternity. Keep your intentions pure and things will fall into place. If you're ever feeling lost or helpless, try even harder to remain true to God's wishes for us.

May 28th

"A peaceful heart leads to a healthy body; jealousy is cancer."

PROVERBS 14:30

There is a strong connection between our mental, emotional, spiritual, and physical health. When we are feeling good spiritually with a joyful and content heart, we receive numerous health benefits physically. But the opposite is also true: a heavy heart will weigh on us physically as well. True peace, joy, and contentment is found in the Lord, so it's essential that we focus our lives on Him. When we focus on living godly lives, our body, mind, and spirit will be unified as one.

May 29th

"Only a fool despises a parent's discipline;
whoever learns from correction is wise."

PROVERBS 15:5

Godly parents correct their children out of love and a
genuine desire to see them reach their full potential. We
would be wise to listen to the advice of godly parents so that we
can become the people God created us to be. God's guidance is
the most important though, as He is our loving Father in heaven
and all knowledge and wisdom belong to Him. A wise person is
much more likely to be humble and open to hearing criticism
from others. As much as we'd like to think, we are not all
knowing. There's always more to learn.

May 30th

"A lazy person's way is blocked with briers, but the path of the upright is an open highway."

PROVERBS 15:19

When we are lazy, it has devastating consequences on our life. The things we are ignoring pile up and we get behind in every area. Then, when we try to catch up, we are continually fighting from behind, constantly encountering obstacles. But when we work hard continuously, the path forward is wide open and full of beautiful opportunities. Get things done early, before they are due. Show up to that appointment five minutes early. Recognize that time is our most valuable asset in life and treat it with the highest respect. Each minute that we lay awake is an opportunity to improve our lives, get more in touch with God and grow spiritually.

May 31st

"Plans go wrong for lack of advice; many advisers bring success."

PROVERBS 15:22

It is foolish to think that we can figure everything out by ourselves. God has created us all as unique individuals with our own experiences, skills, and perspective. When we listen to the advice of others and let them join in our work, whatever we are trying to accomplish just becomes that much better. It's crucial to let others be part of the work you are called to do. They will only enrich it! Don't be afraid to ask for help. Not everyone can read your mind, in fact, nobody can! Put your ego aside, ask for help and enjoy the experience.

June 1ˢᵗ

"Everyone enjoys a fitting reply; it is wonderful
to say the right thing at the right time!"

PROVERBS 15:23

Conversation can be hard. It's challenging to find the right words to say at the right time. But when we do, it's highly beneficial to our relationships! When we live righteously, cultivate wisdom in our hearts, and genuinely listen to others, we will find it easier to uplift them. When we use respectful language and tone to others, it will be met more positively than if we are unkind. Inspire someone else with your words without expecting anything in return. See how you feel.

June 2ⁿᵈ

---

*"If you listen to constructive criticism, you will be
at home among the wise."*

PROVERBS 15:31

Many of us will struggle with criticism of any kind. We can find ourselves defensive and hurt by it. But constructive criticism from godly people holds many benefits! If we humble ourselves, accept the criticism, and choose to work on it appropriately, we will find personal growth like we've never experienced before. Occasionally we are quick to brush away a suggestion made by someone else or refuse to change something we've been working hard on. Step back and see if you can expand your mindset to accommodate the criticisms. Sometimes other people want to lift us up and help us grow to our true potential, not knock us down.

June 3rd

"People may be pure in their own eyes, but the LORD examines their motives."

PROVERBS 16:2

When we practice self-evaluation, we must be careful to judge ourselves according to God's standards and not to our own. We want to ensure that we are living by God's ways. If we only look at our own standards, it's possible that we'll start justifying small sins. These small sins can plant seeds that will eventually overgrow within us. We must begin to take the small wrongdoings just as seriously as the bigger ones. Each sin will start adding up to equal a larger sum.

June 4th

―――――――――――――――――

*"Unfailing love and faithfulness make atonement
for sin. By fearing the Lord, people avoid evil."*

PROVERBS 16:6

Unfailing love and faithfulness are qualities that make up
God's character. When we express those traits in our own
lives, we reflect God in a powerful way. That is exactly what we
need to do to atone for the sins we've committed and find
salvation in Christ. If we continue to walk in this way, fearing
the Lord, we will avoid further sin. We must learn unbounding
respect for God's wishes. Don't be scared to make mistakes, be
scared to not learn from them.

June 5th

"Better to have little, with godliness, than to be rich and dishonest."

PROVERBS 16:8

It's not about the material things we have in this life. It's not about the designer clothing, the fast car, or the mansion at the end of the cul-de-sac. It's all about our character. The stuff we accumulate in this life will not follow us into eternity, but the character we form here will determine our destiny. That means in this life, we must put the focus on how we are living and not on money or possessions. This is how we will arrive in God's eternal Kingdom.

June 6th

"Those who trust the LORD will be joyful."

PROVERBS 16:20

There's a difference between happiness and joy. Happiness is momentary and fleeting, based entirely on the circumstances around us. Let's say that a coworker is thoughtful and brings us a coffee to start our day. That will bring temporary happiness. But joy is different and comes only from God. It persists despite all circumstances and never leaves us. It comes from our full trust in God! Visualize the act of a trust fall, when a person deliberately falls, trusting other members of a group to catch them. God will catch us when we fall. Keep getting back up and strive to do better.

June 7th

"Violent people mislead their companions, leading them down a harmful path."

PROVERBS 16:29

We must be diligent in living godly lives, not just for our own sake, but for the other people around us. The way we live impacts them as well! When we live in a godly way, we help to lead those we love down a secure path. But the same goes the other way. When we live sinful lives, we drag others down in sin with us. Being in a state of rage will risk ruining the lives of those around you as well as your own. Continue to seek other outlets than to be rageful. We can lift weights, go for a run, or take a long relaxing stroll outside. No good will come out of being violent.

June 8th

*"We may throw the dice, but the LORD
determines how they fall."*

PROVERBS 16:33

As people, we tend to desire control in our lives. It makes sense, because we want to ensure that things go well for ourselves and those we love, since we live in a scary world! But we can be okay with not having control. Why? Because God does, and we can trust Him completely with our hearts. We must slowly learn to relinquish control and break free from our stubborn ways. The more we practice living in flow with God, the more stress-free life will seem. Instead of feeling like we must control every outcome, we can simply let things be.

June 9th

"Doing wrong leads to disgrace, and scandalous behavior brings contempt."

PROVERBS 18:3

Our reputation is important. When our reputation is earned, it reflects our character and the way we have lived, treated others, and carried out our business. Good reputation leads to opportunities we would never receive with a bad reputation. If we have earned a bad reputation, all we will receive is disgrace and contempt. Commit to living a godly life and earning a reputation that will bring honor to you and your family. The more we do right in the eyes of God, the more uplifting and supportive we can be for others.

June 10th

---

*"It is not right to acquit the guilty or deny
justice to the innocent."*

PROVERBS 18:5

Much too often, the legal systems of our world unfairly administer justice on both sides of the equation. Those who are guilty roam free sometimes while the innocent sit in prison. There is no excuse for this, and we must be diligent in advocating for a fair and impartial justice system. Keep in mind how this can impact our everyday lives. Be mindful of those wrongfully convicted and pray that their situations be made right, for if this ever happened to us, we would hope others do the same.

June 11ᵗʰ

"A lazy person is as bad as someone who destroys things."

PROVERBS 18:9

This proverb presents us with an interesting analogy. How is a lazy person like someone who destroys things? When we are lazy, we are ignoring important tasks that must be done in our lives. When we neglect important activities, relationships, and work in our lives, those things start to decay. So, in essence, our laziness is destroying them! Commit to working hard in all you do. Work diligently on your passions. Work hard on your relationships, treat them like they are still in the beginning stages when we were all on our best behavior. We all have lazy moments, be aware of them and don't let them take over.

June 12th

*"Spouting off before listening to the facts is both
shameful and foolish."*

PROVERBS 18:13

In our current society, we are quick to speak and slow to listen. This is not good because we start speaking our opinions before we've even heard the whole story! We must commit to being good listeners and think deeply about the facts before offering a reply. Then we will be able to speak with wisdom instead of foolishness and add something insightful to the conversation! It's much easier to react to something out of emotion than it is to maintain composure. Try to take a step back, let both parties present themselves. The truth will always prevail even if it takes more time.

June 13th

"Giving gifts can open doors; it gives access to important people!"

PROVERBS 18:16

This verse doesn't speak to bribes, but rather honest, genuine gift giving from a loving heart. Think of those in your life and how you can bless them with a gift. It will show godly character from you and enrich their lives in a special way. When you do this, you will inspire the same kindness in the other person, creating a ripple effect that will likely come back to bless you in some way! Important people in this proverb could refer to those closest to you. When we give a thoughtful gift, we make someone else feel special.

June 14th

"An offended friend is harder to win back than a fortified city. Arguments separate friends like a gate locked with bars."

PROVERBS 18:19

God has blessed us richly with the gift of friendship. Friends bring so much joy to our lives and we must be careful in always treating them with love and respect. Remember, it's much easier to not say hurtful or cruel words in the first place than it is to try and heal the damage they have done! Commit to cherishing and caring for each one of the friendships God has blessed you with! Sometimes we must be the one to reach out first or initiate most of the plans with our friends. This is okay! Never feel shame for being vulnerable and expressing that you'd like to spend time with someone.

June 15th

"Sensible people control their temper; they earn respect by overlooking wrongs."

PROVERBS 19:11

Our tempers can be hard to control but it's something worth striving for. Lashing out in anger is NEVER the right answer. All it does is create conflict, destroy relationships, and hurt people. When we keep our calm, looking to resolve whatever conflict is at hand, and respond in loving forgiveness, we earn respect and a good reputation with others. Everyone makes mistakes, us included. Why be the person that reacts negatively toward someone else when they make a mistake? It happens. Be a sensible person and overlook the fault the next time someone else is in the wrong.

June 16th

"Unfailing love and faithfulness protect the king;
his throne is made secure through love."

PROVERBS 20:28:

The Bible tells us that God *IS* love. That means everything He is and everything He does reflects what true love is all about! His love is defined by faithfulness to all His people. When we walk honestly with Him, He will always be by our side. We can trust in His promises and rest in His loving presence. When we falter, He will still be there. If we practice remorse for our sins and put our egos aside to ask for forgiveness, He will stay by our side even when the going gets tough.

June 17th

"When arguing with your neighbor, don't betray another person's secret."

PROVERBS 25:9

It's important that we keep secrets that have been entrusted to us. Revealing a secret can irrevocably damage a relationship. Doing so means that we have broken trust and will have an incredibly hard time ever regaining it. When you accept a secret, commit to keeping it. Be the person that can be counted on to keep a sacred piece of information. Just because revealing private information could help you "win" an argument, doesn't mean it's the right thing to do.

June 18th

---

*"Patience can persuade a prince, and soft speech
can break bones."*

PROVERBS 25:15

When we think of strength, we think of aggressive speech
and actions. But the Bible shows us something different.
Loving, wise, and kind words are much more powerful than
hateful or aggressive ones! If we truly want to bring about change
and impact the world, we must do so with godly speech!
Sometimes even saying less will lead to more. Be conscious of the
words you speak, be mindful of how they will influence others.
Take a moment to pause before responding and know that God
will appreciate our effort to improve our communication.

June 19th

"It's not good to eat too much honey, and it's not good to seek honors for yourself."

PROVERBS 25:27

Honor and respect are given, not demanded. When we receive something because we insist on it, it doesn't mean anything! It's much more meaningful and profitable when people give us their honor and respect of their own free will because we have earned it. Live your life in a godly way for the right motives and these blessings will come to you. Take artist Vincent van Gogh for example. His work wasn't recognized during his lifetime. Now, he's regarded as one of the best painters to ever live. Honor and respect will come, but don't sit around waiting for it.

June 20th

*"Don't rejoice when your enemies fall; don't be
happy when they stumble."*

PROVERBS 24:17

God created everyone and loves us all equally. That means
that we shouldn't rejoice at the pain or failures of our
enemies. Instead, we are called to love them just as God does.
When we serve our enemies and show them love, it has a chance
to soften their hearts and bring them back to righteousness. This
is how Jesus lived and how we must also pattern our lives. If we
have the courage, we can attempt to help our enemies in some
way. Perhaps simply by being kind to them. Who knows, maybe
they'll turn into a friend.

June 21st

"My child, fear the LORD and the king. Don't associate with rebels."

PROVERBS 24:21

G od is loving and kind, so we don't have to fear Him harming us. But we must have a healthy reverence and respect for Him that helps motivate us to walk along the right path. God holds all authority and power over this world and our lives. It's best that we live according to His will! When things get tough and we lose motivation, we must remember that God has a plan for us. It's not always going to be clear. It won't always be fun. But He will be there for us. Stay true to His teachings and over time the plan will present itself to you if you trust in Him fully.

June 22nd

"The godly give good advice to their friends; the wicked lead them astray."

PROVERBS 12:26

We have a bigger impact on the lives of others than we realize. Our words influence the lives of others, whether they outright tell us that or not. That's why we must be extremely cautious with the words we speak. We don't ever want to lead anyone astray, but rather toward the love, peace, joy, and eternal life that God so freely gives! The better and honest advice we can give, the more we shall receive in return. We will never regret uplifting someone close to us with a thoughtful piece of guidance.

June 23rd

"Don't wear yourself out trying to get rich. Be wise enough to know when to quit."

PROVERBS 23:4

Many people will chase wealth to the point of exhaustion. They will work an unhealthy number of hours, neglecting so many other important things in life. At the end of it all, their reward is fleeting and not guaranteed. It's best to work hard but respectable hours that allow us time for our family, friends, and most importantly, God Himself. When we are missing dates, family functions or our children's events, we may want to step back and ask ourselves if the work is worth it. We don't want to get to the position in life where we start to lose a part of ourselves because we've overworked.

June 24th

"My child, if your heart is wise, my own heart will rejoice!"

PROVERBS 23:15

God doesn't ask us to follow His ways because He is strict, cruel, or wants to feed His own ego. God wants us to live righteously because He knows the many benefits it will bring to us. He wants us to live joyful, peaceful, and prosperous lives through Him. He knows that kind of life comes through wisdom, so when our hearts are wise, it brings Him genuine joy and He rejoices in us! He always wants what is best for us even if it may not feel like it sometimes. Fill your heart with His love and continue to practice spiritual faith daily.

June 25th

"If you fail under pressure, your strength is too small."

PROVERBS 24:10

This proverb may sound harsh, but we should peel back the layers of meaning to fully comprehend it. When we live godly lives and do preparation for the tasks ahead, we will have strength and perform well under pressure. That's why it's essential that we live our lives with a focus on what is to come so we can be ready for anything thrown our way. We can start by doing small tasks each day to prepare us for tomorrow. Workout longer, cook a healthy meal, spend time with loved ones. Each of these healthy activities will begin to multiply and your mind, body, and spirit will be more prepared for all situations.

June 26th

"Honor is no more associated with fools than snow with summer or rain with harvest."

PROVERBS 26:1

Honor is not seen prominently in our society, and that is a shame. Honor is important because it shows our upright and godly character. These are things to strive for and we must honor those who have them. Living foolishly bears no fruit in our lives. We must seek honor in God's eyes by living according to His will for us. Think of if we practiced living with honor for one week versus living in sin for one week. Which would make us feel better? Which would open more doors for us?

June 27th

"As a door swings back and forth on its hinges, so the lazy person turns over in bed."

PROVERBS 26:14

This proverb speaks against idleness and laziness. When we're lazy, we tend to spend too much time in bed. Restful sleep is necessary, but we must make sure to get up and work hard during the day too. God has prepared a special purpose for each of our lives and if we are to live it out, we must work hard toward it. Encountering sleep issues from time to time is normal. We must be mindful of getting good rest but it's a balance. If we find ourselves laying around too much during the day, we will begin to stray from our intended purpose.

June 28th

"Just as damaging as a madman shooting a deadly weapon is someone who lies to a friend and then says, 'I was only joking.'"

PROVERBS 26:18

We must realize the power of our words and understand that senseless joking and lying is dangerous. That's precisely why the Bible uses such strong language against it in this proverb. When we throw words around carelessly all that results is pain and conflict. We must consider our words carefully before we say them. Words cannot be taken back. They are forever. Sure, we can apologize for saying something mean, but that won't take away the sting that our words can have.

June 29th

"Smooth words may hide a wicked heart, just as a pretty glaze covers a clay pot."

PROVERBS 26:23

In pottery, different designs, glazes, and paints cover up what is a simple clay pot underneath. In the same way, people cover up their sins with fancy words and deceptions. We must be careful to consider the character of a person just as much as the words they say. Pay more attention to someone's actions than their words. People will tell you what you want to hear in an attempt to influence you. Instead of following in their speech, see if they follow it up with actions, or if their words are as empty as a blank stare.

June 30th

"A stone is heavy, and sand is weighty, but the resentment caused by a fool is even heavier."

PROVERBS 27:3

When we live foolishly and not in a God-pleasing manner, we leave a lot of hurt and resentment in our wake. Living ungodly lives brings pain and frustration in our relationships. Those hurt by our sinful patterns end up resenting us. This ends up putting too much weight on everyone's shoulders. Therefore, we must follow God's pattern for how to live out honorable lives. Even if it's one day at a time. We must remain aware of how our small patterns of behavior can snowball and end up turning into an avalanche. Relationships are delicate and must be treated as such. Some can be so rewarding in the beginning, only to crumble to unearthed resentment.

July 1ˢᵗ

*"A person who is full refuses honey, but even
bitter food tastes sweet to the hungry."*

PROVERBS 27:7

We should be grateful for everything the Lord has given us. Not everyone has the chance to eat as we do. Some people don't have their pick of food, or struggle to find food at all. That's why we must be grateful for everything God has blessed us with and pray for those who need God's provision to find the sustenance their bodies need. If you've ever tried to go without food for a prolonged period, you'll be familiar with the state of fragility the body and mind experience while fasting. Keep this in mind during your next meal. Be even more grateful for the food on the table.

July 2nd

"The wicked die and disappear, but the family of the godly stands firm."

PROVERBS 12:7

When we live sinful lives, we do not leave a powerful legacy behind when we pass. We also don't move on to eternal life in God's Kingdom. Our existence is wiped away and we spend eternity in torment. But God gives us a way out of this fate. If we stand on godly principles and follow Him throughout life, we create a powerful legacy here on earth and reap the eternal rewards of His Kingdom! We should all aspire to live godly lives and leave behind legacies we are proud of.

July 3rd

"A prudent person foresees danger and takes precautions. The simpleton goes blindly on and suffers the consequences."

PROVERBS 27:12

As we go through life, it's crucial that we plan and prepare for whatever may be coming ahead. This goes for every area of our lives, from family, to work to ministry. In all these areas, if we take the time necessary to plan and prepare for what's next, we will be much more successful as a result. If we've been inconsistent with reading holy teachings, we could make a goal to read them at least once per week. Or attend a service for an upcoming holiday. The more we plan in all areas, the less anxiety will be present in our daily lives.

July 4th

"Evil people don't understand justice, but those who follow the LORD understand completely."

PROVERBS 28:5

When people live sinful lives, they tend to justify or outright ignore the wicked things they are doing. They will make excuses as to why they continue to sin, blaming just about everyone or everything but themselves. Because of this, justice means nothing to them. They don't believe they deserve it. Since they don't think they've done anything wrong, they feel no need to offer repentance. Sadly, this means salvation won't come to them. One of the best teachings we can learn from God is that we can be forgiven if we are remorseful. Without recognizing our own faults, we will be unable to seek forgiveness.

July 5th

"Blessed are those who fear to do wrong, but the stubborn are headed for serious trouble."

PROVERBS 28:14

Walking in a close and personal relationship with God makes us want to do what is right and fear to do what is wrong. Our relationship with Him makes us genuinely want to please Him and live out the life He has created us for. When we are stubborn and cling to living our own ways, we bring trouble upon ourselves. Sometimes we find it much easier to return to old habits out of comfort. Instead, if we learn to embrace the uncomfortable feeling of change, we will experience new wisdom given from God.

July 6th

---

*"In the end, people appreciate honest criticism
far more than flattery."*

PROVERBS 28:23

It's important for us to be honest with others. Even when it's hard, people genuinely appreciate when we're being real with them. It's obvious when we are being a certain way just to flatter someone, and that can come off as fake or disingenuous. Even if what we have to say is difficult, a wise person will appreciate it and credit you for it. The more we practice being truthful, the more we will attract like-minded people into our lives. People that are dependable, honest, and reliable. The type of people we want to make memories with, share meals with and practice faith with.

July 7th

"Whoever gives to the poor will lack nothing, but those who close their eyes to poverty will be cursed."

PROVERBS 28:27

God rewards our generosity but is saddened when we close our hearts and eyes to those in need. He wants us to give what we can to the poor so that they don't go hungry or cold. God will bless us for being generous. The next time you're in a big city, try giving something to someone in need. Even if it's just a few dollars or a small meal, this could completely transform someone's day. All it takes is one breakthrough act of kindness from a stranger for someone else's world to become brighter.

July 8th

"*I, wisdom, live together with good judgment. I know where to discover knowledge and discernment.*"

PROVERBS 8:12

Wisdom, knowledge, and discernment go hand in hand. There are many times in our lives where we don't know what the right answer is or what we should do next. In those times, we should dive into the knowledge and wisdom God provides. It will show us a clear path forward and give us the strength to see it through. Sometimes when we're really struggling to make a big decision, it could be that we've gotten further away from God. Start small by praying for clarity. You will find it.

July 9th

"My children, listen to me, for all who follow my ways are joyful."

PROVERBS 8:32

In this verse, wisdom speaks. When we follow the wisdom of God, we find true joy in life. This is not fleeting, or momentary joy based upon our circumstances, but everlasting joy rooted in the grace of God. When we live our lives for God, we receive this joy and are blessed by it for the rest of our lives. It may feel like we are delaying our gratification when we make godly choices. This is normal! Instant successes or pleasures will often disappear just as quickly.

July 10th

"Teach the righteous, and they will learn even more."

PROVERBS 9:9

When we choose to live honorably, we have a genuine desire to continue learning about God and His ways. We continually seek wisdom and knowledge, striving to be everything God has created us to be. When we are taught, we listen eagerly and learn as much as humanly possible! We must continue to seek additional knowledge from God. Attempting to expand our minds beyond what we currently know. When we keep learning, we keep growing. We're all students of God, and we're eager to grow together.

July 11th

"If you become wise, you will be the one to benefit. If you scorn wisdom, you will be the one to suffer."

PROVERBS 9:12

We have two choices in life. We can either choose to seek out God's wisdom and live out our lives according to His will, or we can dismiss the Bible and live according to the ways of the world. Trusting God will bring us immeasurable benefits and lead us to salvation, while the other will lead us to ruin and eternal damnation. Which will you choose? This may sound harsh, but religion is being bombarded with attacks in our modern society. Sometimes it's even attacked when we're proud of our faith. Why is that?

July 12th

"A wise child brings joy to a father; a foolish child brings grief to a mother."

PROVERBS 10:1

When we live earning the honor of holy people and most importantly, God Himself, we bring joy to our family. We build upon the reputation of our family name and let the world know that we belong to the Lord. Doing so can impact your family for generations to come. Your children and your children's children will be more likely to come to know the Lord through the way you live your life now! You may not think your present actions will have much impact on the future, but everything we do today will have a direct correlation on our day tomorrow.

July 13th

"A wise youth harvests in the summer."

PROVERBS 10:5

This proverb contains farming language, speaking to the planting, cultivating, and harvesting of crops. Even though many of us today don't farm, the logic here still applies. We reap what we sow. If we work hard now, it will pay off abundantly later! Just because you can't always see the fruit of what you're doing right now, keep up the hard work and it will pay off before you know it. Usually, the best type of work brings a future reward. Not an instant hit of dopamine.

July 14th

"People who accept discipline are on the pathway to life, but those who ignore correction will go astray."

PROVERBS 10:17

This proverb presents a bold statement, but one that couldn't be truer. Instead of becoming defensive when offered criticism, what if we honestly evaluated ourselves in wake of it and strived to be better? This is how we grow in life! There's always room to grow and be better! Think of a time where you experienced vast personal growth. Was it in a time of hardship? Going through difficult times leads to greater strength and discipline. If you're going through something difficult, stick with it. The payoff will be greater.

July 15th

"The words of the godly encourage many, but fools are destroyed by their lack of common sense."

PROVERBS 10:21

When we walk in a personal relationship with God, we have a natural desire to share the Bible with everyone we meet! When we do, we bring encouragement to more people than we know. You never know how hearing the Gospel can change someone's life. This is a task we are called to and must stick to it to avoid becoming a fool without common sense, spreading meaningless words instead of the Gospel. It doesn't mean we have to shout our knowledge out from the rooftops but share one of your favorite passages or proverbs with someone close to you. See how they respond.

July 16th

*"Discipline your children while there is hope.
Otherwise, you will ruin their lives."*

PROVERBS 19:18

Because of our fallen nature, we tend to do wrong. We see this in children who are too young to comprehend what right and wrong is. That's why we must be diligent in teaching them from an early age, so they can grow up knowing the Lord instead of following their human nature into a life of sin. We have the power to shape our children via our actions. If we have lazy habits, chances are the children will too. If we lead disciplined and godly lives, chances are the children will too.

July 17th

"The lips of the godly speak helpful words, but the mouth of the wicked speaks perverse words."

PROVERBS 10:32

We should desire to help and encourage our fellow human beings. We are all God's children who He loves equally and unconditionally. Considering this, it's important to be conscious of the way we speak. Commit to speaking helpful and honest words, and you will truly impact the lives of others. Next time you are in a tense conversation, try and inject some nice words into the dialogue. It's okay to speak bluntly but do so in a kind way. There is no benefit to anyone when using hateful words.

July 18th

"The LORD detests the use of dishonest scales,
but He delights in accurate weights."

PROVERBS 11:1

The way of the godly is to always be honest and fair. We must never manipulate or be dishonest in any situation to gain an advantage for ourselves. When we do this, we are disobeying God. Being honest and fair must be a bigger priority in our life than anything else. Think about visiting an honest business versus a business that misrepresents products and goods. Which would you be more likely to return to?

July 19th

"The godly are directed by honesty; the wicked fall beneath their load of sin."

PROVERBS 11:5

We must commit our lives to honesty in the Lord. When we do, He will guide us through the highs and lows. What will He guide us to? Opportunities, godly relationships, joy, and peace. This type of life contrasts a sinful one, where the combined weight of our sin keeps us stuck in the same place. Commit to reaching the fullness of your potential in God through an honest life! Anything short of honest and we fall short of our potential. We can make a profound difference in our lives if we start by being honest with ourselves and others. Everything else will fall into place.

July 20th

"It is foolish to belittle one's neighbor; a sensible person keeps quiet."

PROVERBS 11:12

Hurtful, unkind, or hateful words are never the answer, even if someone has committed an injustice against us. In those instances, it is much more respectful to keep quiet. It's just like the old saying, "If you've got nothing nice to say, don't say anything at all." It's much better to say nothing than to say things you can't take back. Our neighbors share a similar journey to us. They have highs and lows just like we do. Sure, we may get annoyed with them from time to time, but it's best to let things go. Be kind and form good relationships with them.

July 21st

"Evil people get rich for the moment, but the reward of the godly will last."

PROVERBS 11:18

We might get confused when we see evil people prospering in life. We may start to question if their way of life is right and ours is wrong. But we must remember that the wealth and prestige they gain through such means is temporary and fleeting. The reward we receive for living a godly life is eternal! When we stay committed to a holy life, our rewards will be far greater. One doesn't need to flaunt such rewards on social media. We can quietly thank God for everything we have and all that we will receive.

July 22nd

"People curse those who hoard their grain, but they bless the one who sells in time of need."

PROVERBS 11:26

In our society today, we are taught to hoard things for the future. We do it to comfort ourselves and build up a sense of security. But our security can't come from doing such things. Our security must rest solely in the Lord. When we give generously for the sake of others, God blesses us and makes sure we have everything we need. A false sense of security is a dangerous concept. Any perceived security is temporary. The only true security we have in life is from God's love.

July 23rd

*"The LORD approves of those who are good,
but He condemns those who plan wickedness."*

PROVERBS 12:2

We should desire nothing more in this life than the approval of God. He is our loving Father in heaven who created us from an overflow of His love. His approval is worth more than any amount of money, fame, or prestige in this life. Through His approval, we are granted eternal life in His Kingdom marked by everlasting peace, love, and joy. What better reward could we receive than that?

July 24th

"If sinners entice you, turn your back on them!"

PROVERBS 1:10

As God's children, it's only natural that we would want to welcome everybody with open arms and give our time to them. But it's important to be selective on who we get close with. When we keep the company of sinners too closely, they impact our lives in negative ways, drawing us into their sin. If they will not turn from their sin, it's good to keep your distance! The same can be applied for your children's lives too. Don't be easily influenced by sinners. Practice self-control and avoid them when necessary.

July 25th

"A fool is quick-tempered, but a wise person stays calm when insulted."

PROVERBS 12:16

Have you ever known someone who had a bad temper? They are stressful to be around! You must tread carefully, making sure not to set them off about something. We must have a strong base in the Lord to not be emblematic of them. All we do when we lash back against someone is discredit ourselves. Wisdom will stifle conflicts before they even start. Try continuing being kind to the ill-tempered individual. They may be going through something we don't know about. But don't let them cast their wicked ways onto you. Be above their negativity by being calm.

July 26th

---

*"Some people make cutting remarks, but the
words of the wise bring healing."*

PROVERBS 12:18

Our words are powerful, and we'd be wise to remember that. Through our words, we can hurt or heal. When we attack, criticize, and say hurtful things toward others, we wound them. But when we encourage, empower, and teach others, we bring deep healing to their souls. It's like how our body heals when we are kind to it with rest. The same can be said about speaking kind words to others. We will uplift them and speak directly to their souls with thoughtful words. Cutting remarks however will lead to other negative actions and sins.

July 27th

"The wise don't make a show of their knowledge, but fools broadcast their foolishness."

PROVERBS 12:23

When we find wisdom and contentment in the Lord, we also find humbleness. We don't feel the need to make ourselves look wise and smart to others. All the joy we need is found in reaping the benefits of God's wisdom! But those who are foolish will make a show of themselves, no matter how unwise and sinful they are. We can trust in ourselves and God that we are wise. We can trust that we are on the right path and are constantly wanting to learn more about God and all that he has created for us. Why showboat on social media to appease mere strangers?

July 28th

"Speak up for those who cannot speak for themselves; ensure justice for those being crushed."

PROVERBS 31:8

There are people in this world, considering their poverty or social influence in life, that don't have the same opportunities as we do. But we must realize that God doesn't care about worldly wealth or social status. He loves each one of His children all the same. That's why we must use our voice to advocate on behalf of those in need. In doing so, we'll show them the love of Christ. Those less fortunate than us could need help but may be shy to ask for it. When you see someone in need, offer to help in whatever way you can. Spend time with them, buy them a hot cup of coffee or tea or speak kind words to them.

July 29th

"Those who control their tongue will have a long life; opening your mouth can ruin everything."

PROVERBS 13:3

Being careful with the words we speak can make or break our lives. Using kind and thoughtful words will lead us to important relationships and a multitude of opportunities. But speaking unkindly or out of turn can take all those opportunities and relationships away in a moment! Being kind is one of the most common themes among the proverbs. Sure, it may be simple advice. But the simplest actions repeated over and over can lead to the biggest and longest-lasting results. Controlling our tongue and being thoughtful with our spoken word will benefit ourselves just as much as someone else.

July 30th

"The rich can pay a ransom for their lives, but the poor won't even get threatened."

PROVERBS 13:8

While it may not seem like it to many people, living with less can be a huge blessing. The more we have, the more there is to worry about. We end up becoming consumed by our earthly possessions! But when we are content to live a simpler life, we find joy in the small things, just as we were created to do. We will then be able to focus on God, family, and friends! The less we have, the more grateful we are for each thing in our lives. We can try living beneath our means for a few months and what matters most to us will shine even brighter.

July 31st

"Good people leave an inheritance to their grandchildren, but the sinner's wealth passes to the godly."

PROVERBS 13:22

The legacy we leave will ultimately define us. What will we pass on to future generations of our family? The way we live today will determine the answer to that question. That's why it's crucial that we cling to the Lord and follow His guidance through life. Think of the life you wish you had growing up. Use that as motivation to work hard for the next generation after you. Leave plenty for them so that they have the freedom to explore their own journey in life. Maybe they want to attend art school or play sports as an example, leaving them ample resources will help them to follow their dreams.

August 1st

"A wise woman builds her home, but a foolish woman tears it down with her own hands."

PROVERBS 14:1

God gives us each the opportunity to build a beautiful life or to destroy it. He gives us this free will because He loves us, and there is no love without free will. When we choose to build a good life, He helps us and guides us every step of the way. All we must do is ask Him to give us the gift of the Holy Spirit and follow where He leads. In our modern society, it's looked down upon to be labeled as a homemaker. Why? Being a full-time mother is one of the most important and fulfilling lines of work there is. Perhaps it's that people tend to speak negatively about things they are jealous of.

August 2nd

*"Stay away from fools, for you won't find
knowledge on their lips."*

PROVERBS 14:7

The company we keep can have a massive impact on our
lives. When we surround ourselves with wise and godly
people, we learn from them, becoming wise and godly ourselves.
Yet the same is true on the flip side. When we hang around bad
influences, they rub off on us. Commit to finding a community
of believers where you can find beneficial fellowship! Be a role
model among your peers and help them achieve new heights. Use
your wisdom and godly knowledge to help them reach their goals
and dreams.

August 3rd

*"Fools make fun of guilt, but the godly
acknowledge it and seek reconciliation."*

PROVERBS 14:9

We all mess up sometimes. It's normal to do something wrong at some point in your life. In those instances, the right thing to do is to acknowledge our mistakes and seek to make things right. When we do that, our sins are covered by the grace of Jesus, and we have the blessed opportunity to restore a relationship and bring healing to another's heart. We also must learn to forgive ourselves for our mistakes. Carrying around guilt and shame will be of no benefit to us. We must be remorseful but move forward and leave our past mistakes behind us.

August 4th

*"Backsliders get what they deserve; good people
receive their reward."*

PROVERBS 14:14

The simple truth of life is that what we receive is based on what we put in. When we live honest and hard-working lives, we receive the benefits of that lifestyle. When we don't, we only get the punishment we have brought upon ourselves. The Bible makes it clear what to expect when we choose to live this way, so we only have ourselves to blame! If we wake up and aim to make each day better than the previous, we will be far better off one year from the present day.

August 5th

"Corrupt people walk a thorny, treacherous road;
whoever values life will avoid it."

PROVERBS 22:5

When we live corruptly, we only make our journey through life more difficult. While it may seem like shortcuts are making things easier in the present, they only compound our problems down the road. The shortcuts we take today make things far more difficult for us in the future. But if we live justly, we will follow an even, steady path. Be wary of shortcuts that sound too good to be true like get rich quick schemes. Often, it's the long and trusted road that will bring results. Continue to have patience and put your trust in God, good things are on the way to you!

August 6th

"Just as the rich rule the poor, so the borrower is servant to the lender."

PROVERBS 22:7

We must be careful with what kind of debts we allow ourselves to take out. While the deal may seem good at the moment, being in debt to another can put us in a challenging situation. We end up being bound to that lender until we pay back the entirety of the loan. It's much better to have freedom in our finances. Credit cards offer intriguing perks. But it's easy to rack up debt with interest accumulating on it. Live within your means and try spending only out of necessity.

August 7th

"The godly are rescued from trouble, and it falls on the wicked instead."

PROVERBS 11:8

Our planet is filled with many troubles since sin entered the world in the Garden of Eden. When we live godly lives, God grants us a shield of protection to help us through the troubles of life. But when we are sinful, we invite trouble right to our door. Choose the holy path and accept God's shelter from the storm. When we do so, it will be a beacon of light during a dark storm at sea. Even when things look bleak, we must always remember that God is here for us. He's watching, listening, and guiding us to a better life.

August 8th

"The king's heart is like a stream of water directed by the LORD; He guides it wherever He pleases."

PROVERBS 21:1

If we are to live our lives correctly, we must have them guided by the Lord. When we live our lives like this, God flows with us like the waters in which He created. This is what we were created for, to live life in perfect unison with God. When we struggle so greatly for control and try to do things our own way, we only turn against God's natural design for us. Try not to swim against the current of the water, life will be much easier. Self-sabotage is a term that comes to mind here. Why make things harder for yourself than they must be?

August 9th

"The violence of the wicked sweeps them away, because they refuse to do what is just."

PROVERBS 21:7

Sin has a way of overtaking our lives and sweeping us away under its influence. The more we engage in it, the more we lose ourselves and succumb to its continual influence. That's why we must saturate ourselves in prayer and the reading of God's Word, the Holy Bible. When we do, we will find protection against the devastating consequences of sin in our lives. When we go a few weeks without sin, it's much easier to keep the streak going. But if we constantly slip up day to day, we are going to have many more obstacles to face when trying to leave our sins behind.

August 10th

"Those who love pleasure become poor; those who love wine and luxury will never be rich."

PROVERBS 21:17

If we are to build up wealth in this life, we must be careful with our finances. If we spend all our money on pleasures in this life, we will never gain the financial security we desire. But if we live simpler lives and enjoy the natural blessings of life, we will be able to save and gain wealth much more easily. While it may be hard in the moment, in the end we'll be glad we did! Think of how easy it is to keep spinning a slot machine in Las Vegas. It's much more difficult to work hard and stay patient.

August 11th

"The wise conquer the city of the strong and level the fortress in which they trust."

PROVERBS 21:22

The wisdom we receive from God gives us unmatched strength, the likes of which we can receive nowhere else. This strength can help us defeat any enemy that comes before us. When the devil plots his schemes against us, we can stand strongly and achieve victory in the name of the Lord. The more we build up our metaphorical fortress walls, the less likely evil is to breach. Continue to put your faith in God, work on strengthening your fortress and life will be more rewarding.

August 12th

"Some people are always greedy for more, but the godly love to give!"

PROVERBS 21:26

Being in a relationship with God means that we unite with His mission. He is a giving God and desires that we would pattern ourselves after His example. God blesses us richly when we give from a gracious heart. We must approach giving with the right motives, not seeking glory for ourselves but rather doing it as a genuine response to knowing God. It's like making an anonymous donation to your church or charity of choice. We don't need accolades or praise to do it. We should love giving and expect nothing in return for it. God will praise us for this.

August 13th

*"The horse is prepared for the day of battle, but
the victory belongs to the LORD."*

PROVERBS 21:31

The Lord is all-powerful and can conquer any foe. That's why we want Him to be on our side! He will not hesitate to fight for us and leverage His mighty power against our enemy. He loves us more than we could ever know and will fight for us continually, just as a parent would wield all their strength for their own child. If we ask for His help in defeating the evil in our lives, He will show us the way.

August 14th

"Don't waste your breath of fools, for they will despise the wisest advice."

PROVERBS 23:9

We only have so much time in a day, so it's important that we spend it wisely. We are called to speak truth, love, and encouragement into the lives of others, but we must be wise in spending our time with those who listen to our advice. If people reject our message, it's time to move on to someone who will open their hearts to what we have to say. People learn from their own mistakes. Speaking wise words to someone in an attempt to prevent them from making a mistake, will usually result in a wasted effort. Others, who refuse to listen, will have to make mistakes to learn. They may even come back to you and let you know that you were right all along.

August 15th

"The words of the wicked are like a murderous ambush, but the words of the godly save lives."

PROVERBS 12:6

Hurtful words by sinful people can wound others deeply and lead them down a dark path themselves. There is no excuse for this kind of speech in our lives. Rather, we must commit to speaking wise, life-saving words: the message of the Gospel that leads to eternal life with God! The proverbs are an excellent resource on how to improve our lives. With similar themes being repeated, they stress how important it is for us to practice what we preach: kindness! It's like siblings who grew up bickering with each other, only to learn later in life that they couldn't live without each other's kindness and support.

August 16th

*"Get the truth and never sell it; also get wisdom,
discipline, and good judgment."*

PROVERBS 23:23

G od offers us so many blessings. Among them are truth,
wisdom, discipline, and good judgment. All these things
work together to produce righteousness in our lives. Truth helps
us understand the world, wisdom teaches us how to live,
discipline helps us live it out, and good judgment guides us along
the way. Through prayer, ask God to fill your heart with all these
blessings.

August 17th

"My son, give me your heart. May your eyes take delight in following my ways."

PROVERBS 23:26

God desires nothing more than your heart. He created you to love and be loved by Him. Just as a parent wants their child to follow in their ways, so too does God want us to follow Him in every way! He desires to be an intimate part of our everyday life and share all His love with us. When we experience this with Him, we find joy in following His ways. Think of your day today, how can you let God into your heart? Would He be happy with how your day went? If not, let's ask for His forgiveness and strive to do better tomorrow.

August 18th

---

*"Don't gaze at the wine, seeing how red it is,
how it sparkles in the cup, how smoothly it goes
down. For in the end, it bites like a poisonous
snake; it stings like a viper."*

PROVERBS 23:31-32

Drinking can be dangerous. While it seems fun and we may experience peer pressure from our social group to do it, it's best that we resist the urge to over consume it. Willpower can help us drink responsibly but be cautious about it becoming habitual. We should seek to form positive habits in life like reading, exercising, and spending quality time with family. Drinking is okay in moderation but can get out of control quickly. That's why if we have more than we should, our body lets us know the following day with a hangover. The same for any other substance. The proverbs like to remind us of how over consuming too many pleasures in life can lead to ruin.

August 19th

"*Don't envy evil people or desire their company.*"

PROVERBS 24:1

Sometimes we look at people who are not following the Lord and envy things about their lives. We must be careful in this, because even though parts of their lives seem attractive on the outside, we must remember that what we have in the Lord is much better. The love of God cannot be replaced by any worldly pleasure! We will glow much brighter when we follow God. We will radiate positivity, love, and happiness. This is infinitely more desirable than envying what we see of others on social media.

August 20th

"Rescue those who are unjustly sentenced to die;
save them as they stagger to their death."

PROVERBS 24:11

While our God is a god of justice, He is also a God of mercy. When we are willing to repent our sins and turn back toward Him, He will save us and bring us eternal salvation in His Kingdom. He desires that we would show mercy to others as well, emulating the example of Christ and practicing forgiveness. Everyone is going to make mistakes. Even those closest to you. Be like God and show mercy to them. Forgive the people in your life for their wrongdoings. Use this as an opportunity to get closer to them and be there for them in their time of need.

August 21ˢᵗ

"The wicked take secret bribes to pervert the court of justice."

PROVERBS 17:23

Justice is important to God because He is righteous. He hates to see honest people suffer at the hands of the wicked. Their corrupt nature hurts others. God defends them, and He wishes that we'd rise and do the same. We must also bear honest witness that will help bring righteous judgment in the world. We must stand up for the cause of the poor, oppressed, and innocent. This way of life will please God. It's easy to get distracted by what we read or watch on the news. There's so much corruption it's impossible to completely tune it out. Instead of dwelling on it, feel sorry for the corrupt. They've compromised their lives for immediate pleasure-seeking behavior. Justice will catch up to them, despite how above the law they may think they are.

August 22nd

"It is God's privilege to conceal things and the king's privilege to discover them."

PROVERBS 25:2

God does things on His own timing. He has a limitless perspective that we could never comprehend, and He knows the perfect time for everything. Since He is all-knowing and we are not, we must trust in His timing and wait patiently for His revelations. There are things He will conceal for a time but will joyfully reveal to us when the time is right. Continue exploring with God in mind. Say yes to things you would have previously said no to! Learn to live in a godly way outside your comfort zone, and more will be shown to you.

August 23rd

"Remove the impurities from silver, and the sterling will be ready for the silversmith."

PROVERBS 25:4

G od is often likened to the process of pottery, molding and shaping us from the inside out as we walk with Him through life. Just as silver is purified to be shaped into its final form, so too does God remove the impurities from us to bring us to our full potential. We must trust God with this process and rest assured that He will reveal every beautiful quality He placed within us when He created us.

August 24th

"Valid criticism is like a gold earring or other gold jewelry."

PROVERBS 25:12

If we are to become everything that we can be in life, we must be good and patient listeners. If we aren't willing to accept honest criticism or ever admit to our faults, we won't be able to grow, plain and simple. This is why the Bible speaks so strongly about being humble. Humbleness will lead us to growth like we've never known before. Criticism can take a rusty piece of jewelry and polish it to an even more beautiful design. Instead of being offended by criticism, let's be humble and try to find some truth in what was suggested to us.

August 25th

"As surely as a north wind brings rain, so a gossiping tongue causes anger!"

PROVERBS 25:23

Nothing productive or fruitful comes from gossip. There is no reason to do so as it only causes harm. When we engage in gossip, we are asking for conflict in our relationships. It's much easier to avoid conflict than to resolve it. We can't take away hurtful things we say. We must flee from all gossip in our lives! It's just another bad habit that once started, is difficult to break. There are so many beautiful things to speak about. Why focus on minute details of other people's lives?

August 26th

*"A proverb in the mouth of a fool is as useless as
a paralyzed leg."*

PROVERBS 26:7

We've been studying proverbs and drawing out the wisdom we find within. But proverbs are only fruitful in our lives if we live out the truth we learn from them. If we don't apply their wisdom to our lives, they've done no good for us. As we continue looking at the proverbs, we should find a way to put each one to use to better our lives. Take small parts and themes from the proverbs and slowly apply them to your everyday life. Rewrite ones that apply to you, some may not. But the one's that stick with you can transform your life for the better.

August 27th

"Interfering in someone else's argument is as foolish as yanking a dog's ear."

PROVERBS 26:17

Consider for a moment yanking a dog's ear. Not a good idea, is it? Why aren't we as cautious about interfering in the arguments of others? All we do in that instance is pour more fuel on the fire. Why intensify someone else's problems and make them our own? It is not our business why other people are having conflict. The best we can do is to set a positive example by spreading kindness and godly love in our communities.

August 28th

"A lying tongue hates its victims, and flattering words cause ruin."

PROVERBS 26:28

You can't be loving and lie to someone at the same time. When you deceive another person, you are committing a hateful action against them. If you truly care about someone, you will tell them the truth no matter how difficult it is. You will cherish the relationship you share above any other motivation in your heart. Yes, the truth has the potential to hurt someone else. But that's much less likely if you are acting pure and trustworthy in your relationships. We shouldn't fear telling the truth if we have acted in the best interest of God throughout our daily lives.

August 29th

"Fools are destroyed by their own complacency."

PROVERBS 1:32

We must be careful to never stop learning and growing in life. If we become complacent, we will grow lazy and fall into sin more easily. No one is perfect, so we all have room to grow in our spiritual quests. Spend daily time on the Bible and prayer. These two disciplines will help you grow like never before! Our purpose in work and relationships can change over time. That is okay. Embrace the change but reject complacency. Keep listening to God and continue forward with your journey.

August 30th

"As workers who tend a fig tree are allowed to eat the fruit, so workers who protect their employer's interests will be rewarded."

PROVERBS 27:18

When we are hired to do a job, we must take the responsibility seriously. When we work hard and are loyal to our employer, we will be rewarded appropriately. So many people continuously complain about their jobs and take the opportunity for granted. Instead of following that example, choose to be grateful for the work you've been given and strive to do your work to the best of your ability. Even if you don't like your job or your employer, there's a valuable lesson to be learned. Continue to take the role seriously until your next purpose presents itself.

August 31st

"Know the state of your flocks, and put your heart into caring for your herds."

PROVERBS 27:23

There are times in our lives when we will find ourselves in a leadership position of some sort. When we do, it's crucial that we care for the people who've been entrusted to us. We must work in their best interests in all we do and faithfully serve alongside them in our common mission. It could be parenting. It could be at work or in our church communities. Whenever we are entrusted as leaders, we must make it one of our top priorities to look after those who follow along with us. Lift them up when they are down. Guide them when they are lost. And love them when they are hurt.

September 1st

"A poor person who oppresses the poor is like a pounding rain that destroys the crops."

PROVERBS 28:3

Rain is supposed to hydrate the earth and feed the crops. But when the rain comes too fast and hard, crops are destroyed instead of cultivated. When we oppress people who struggle with the same things we do, we are just like the pounding rain. Instead of lifting up others who can relate to us, we hurt them even further instead. Why not practice God's teachings and attempt to uplift every person we encounter in our lives? It won't work on everyone, but we have the chance to help someone in a meaningful way.

September 2nd

"Young people who obey the law are wise; those with wild friends bring shame to their parents."

PROVERBS 28:7

Sometimes it's hard to find wisdom when we are young. In our youth, we are more easily seduced by our passions and follow our own ways. But the earlier we can start walking along God's path the better. Then we will build a firm foundation that will help carry us through the rest of our lives. We will make mistakes in our youth. And even when we are older too! But it's especially important to cultivate good habits when we are growing up. The better habits we get used to doing now, the stronger we will be as we age.

September 3rd

"Rich people may think they are wise, but a poor person with discernment can see right through them."

PROVERBS 28:11

Wealth and fame can blind us quickly. We will think that because we have money and influence that we must be very wise. It doesn't work that way. There are many poor people who are wiser than any rich person. We must remember to never judge a book by its cover, especially by their financial status. This proverb is becoming increasingly easier to see with the prevalence of social media. Some people with large followings and an abundance of wealth are having a difficult time hiding their true colors.

September 4th

"A murderer's tormented conscience will drive him into the grave. Don't protect Him!"

PROVERBS 28:17

When we approve of, or cover up the sins of others, we are just as guilty as they are. We must attempt to lead others toward repentance instead of helping them conceal their sins. We want to find salvation in Jesus and not drag ourselves down with the misdeeds of others. Everyone will make mistakes in this life. Everyone will sin occasionally. Encourage others to repent and ask for forgiveness of their sins. But know where to draw the line. If someone doesn't want to change their ways, don't get stuck in an endless cycle trying to protect them.

September 5th

"Greedy people try to get rich quick but don't realize they're headed for poverty."

PROVERBS 28:22

Everywhere you look, it seems as if someone has a "get rich quick" scheme. If these worked so well, wouldn't everybody be doing them? We must be careful not to cut corners like this because it will always catch up with us. If we work hard and honestly for our money, we will have a steady income and be able to provide for our needs. It's wise to start business ventures if you have plenty of good ideas that can better peoples' lives. But don't set out with the wrong intentions. Create something that will leave a lasting impact on others. Worry about the returns later.

September 6th

"When the godly are in authority, the people rejoice. But when the wicked are in power, they groan."

PROVERBS 29:2

People rejoice when the godly come to power because they know they will be met with kindness, justice, and prosperity. They know their voices will be heard and that their needs will be taken care of when possible. But when the unrighteous are in charge, the opposite will happen. They think only of themselves, exploiting the people they are called to serve.

September 7th

"The man who loves wisdom brings joy to his father, but if he hangs around with prostitutes, his wealth is wasted."

PROVERBS 29:3

Sexual immorality can get us into trouble in various ways. It can destroy us physically, emotionally, spiritually, and financially. It will ruin our relationships and twist our personal character. God has designed sexual expression for its own time and place. If we want to experience the real thing by God's design instead of a cheap imitation, we should respect God's guidance in this area. Of course, it's not always possible, but it's the idea that should be kept sacred and we should attempt to honor it when able.

September 8th

"To flatter friends is to lay a trap for their feet."

PROVERBS 29:5

Flattery is not the way to go about honoring others. Flattery is a deception meant to win the good favor of someone else when we have ulterior motives. If we desire to praise someone, we must not do it for selfish gain, instead only from the sincerity of our hearts. Then we will truly be honoring them and building them up in the name of the Lord. We can practice giving compliments in the spur of the moment. Think of things you're grateful for about someone in your life that you love. Let them know! Remind them how blessed you are to have them in your life.

September 9th

"The bloodthirsty hate blameless people, but the
upright seek to help them."

PROVERBS 29:10

Sadly, there are many people in this world who are malicious and seek to harm others. One tactic that helps is to love and serve these people despite their poor intentions. When we do, we can often diffuse their hostility and bring about a change in them as they see a different power at work within us. We've all met someone who is consistently negative or moody. Perhaps they have something going on that we aren't privy to knowing about. We can still attempt to help them by being kind. With persistent kindness, you'd be surprised at how much someone can open up. They may even have something special waiting behind their closed doors.

September 10th

"If a ruler pays attention to liars, all his advisers will be wicked."

The company we keep can have an ill effect on our reputation. If people see us associating with liars and morally corrupt people, we will start to attract more of the same. We want to encourage godly people to be near us instead. Their encouragement and guidance will help us to grow in every way. It's the same if we surround ourselves with negative people. What's likely to come of us?

September 11th

"When people do not accept divine guidance, they run wild. But whoever obeys the law is joyful."

PROVERBS 29:18

God is always trying to get our attention in both big and small ways. He wants to guide our lives! Why? Because He desires to see you prosper and He knows exactly how to get you there. But often, we don't recognize His presence in our lives. When that happens, we don't follow the path He has set before us. We must open our eyes to His presence so He can lead us to true and everlasting joy. It's a lot easier to see the evil in our lives than all the blessings God puts before us. It's like the adage that it's easier to be negative than positive. We might have to pay more attention because He's always around us trying to bring joy to our lives!

September 12th

"Pride ends in humiliation, while humility brings honor."

PROVERBS 29:23

When we are prideful, all we do is bring shame upon ourselves. Our pride leads to us making foolish and useless decisions. These decisions lead our lives down an embarrassing path that humiliates us. That's exactly why we should walk in humility. With humility comes a well-lived life that brings us honor among all, most importantly God Himself. It's okay to be proud of our accomplishments, but there's no need to gloat about them. We'll be recognized for our efforts when the time is right. In the meantime, we should strive to remain humble.

September 13th

"Many seek the ruler's favor, but justice comes from the LORD."

PROVERBS 29:26

No matter where we live, we will find ourselves living under some sort of government. No matter who it is that's governing us, it's beneficial to be on their good side so that we can reap the benefits of their influence. But at the end of the day, we must remember that true power and authority belongs only to God Himself. He has more authority than any earthly ruler so He should always be our number one. Government will always be ebbing and flowing. History does tend to repeat itself, there's no need to get caught up in the daily negativity surrounding politics. Stand up for whatever you believe in and give thanks to God!

September 14th

"The righteous despise the unjust; the wicked despise the godly."

PROVERBS 29:27

We are living during a spiritual battleground between the forces of God and Satan. In this war, there is no middle ground: we must take a side. If we do not choose to fight on the side of God, we have chosen to align ourselves with the devil. While we should preach to the unjust and try to lead them to repentance, we must be careful not to get too close. The best thing we can do is continue to lead by example. Show others what living a godly life looks like. Prioritize family and raising children. Support your local community. Those might not seem like ways of participating in the "war," but they will go a long way in strengthening your faith.

September 15th

"Every word of God proves true. He is a shield to all who come to Him for protection."

PROVERBS 30:5

The Holy Bible contains God's very words, passed down to the biblical authors who transcribed them for us. Throughout the Scriptures, we see many promises from God. We can rest assured that each one will come true. God is the very definition of what it means to be faithful and true to His word. He will protect us against all evil and defend us in every way. It may not always be abundantly clear, but He is always watching! He is always with us. And He is trying to show us how to live our best lives.

September 16ᵗʰ

"Give me neither poverty nor riches! Give me just enough to satisfy my needs."

PROVERBS 30:8

The Bible says that money is the root of all evil. The reason for this is that it has caused people to commit sins in its name. It can consume us and begin to control us. That's why we must never place money above God. We must echo this prayer, asking God to give us enough to live but not more than we need before it influences our lives in a negative way. Starting a new venture solely with profits in mind, is likely to unravel quickly. Instead, start the money-generating venture with helping others in mind. The business will likely flourish and bring about much more than profit.

September 17th

"They are pure in their own eyes, but they are filthy and unwashed."

PROVERBS 30:12

We must be careful to maintain a healthy and honest perception of ourselves. If we justify our sins and think of ourselves as innocent even when we're in need of Christ's salvation, we'll never grow. When we think this way, we are never driven toward repentance. But the truth is that we always need the Lord! Never be shy to ask for help. Whether it's a trusted friend or someone in your faith community, have the humility to admit when you need help. If we're able to communicate our needs with others, God will hear our prayers and help present solutions in our lives.

September 18th

"Such is the fate of all who are greedy for money; it robs them of life."

PROVERBS 1:19

When the Bible speaks of idols, we may think only of statues made in an image of another God. This doesn't sound very relevant to us today, does it? Well, idols are more than statues. Idols are anything that take the place of God in our hearts. Money is a common one, and we must be careful to never get too greedy for it. Each day on Earth is a precious gift from God. Why squander every day obsessing about monetary gain? Ideally, we will find purpose in our working lives without letting them be all consuming of our precious time and energy.

September 19th

"He grants a treasure of common sense to the honest. He is a shield to those who walk with integrity."

PROVERBS 2:7

There are many voices in this world constantly trying to bombard us with their opinion of what we should believe is right and wrong. But there is only one truth, and it's to be found in the Lord. When we commit to Him, He grants us this common sense and clears our minds for godly discernment. If you ever question whether something is right or wrong, consult the bible or any other source of God's wisdom. Typically, if we must question if something in our lives is right or wrong, it's a sign that it's not right. This may be God's way of nudging us to go in another direction.

September 20th

*"She has abandoned her husband, and ignores
the covenant she made before God."*

PROVERBS 2:17

Marriage is a serious, holy, and beautiful thing in God's eyes. We must likewise treat it with all respect and reverence. When we do, we honor not only our spouse, but God Himself. A promise made before God to be faithful to your spouse is not something to be taken lightly. God will not recognize or honor any of the actions you take that drive you away from your partner. You will be in sin. Affairs are made to look glamorous on TV, but what are they actually? They end up ruining the lives of others and destroying something that was once sacred.

September 21st

*"The wicked will be removed from the land,
and the treacherous will be uprooted."*

PROVERBS 2:22

When we walk with the Lord, we walk under His protection in this dark and twisted world. But when we live wickedly, we choose to cast away that protection. We are uprooted from the blessing of God's Kingdom and left to our own means. But it's all our choice! That's why we must choose to walk with God! It's an active choice to attempt to do our best each day. To wake up and begin our day offering thanks to God for yet an opportunity to make an impact in this world. Whether it's around our house, at work, or with a loved one, each day presents moments for us to share God's wisdom with one another.

September 22nd

"Never let loyalty and kindness leave you! Tie them around your neck as a reminder. Write them deep within your heart."

PROVERBS 3:3

L oyalty and kindness are two traits that closely mirror God's very own character. That's why we must keep them close. When we keep them at the forefront of our hearts and minds, we will naturally respond to people with them. This is what we must endeavor for! Being loyal is one of the highest honors you can give to a loved one, a co-worker or a friend. Being supportive of those around you, regardless of what you are going through, is the best way to spread God's message to those who need it most.

September 23rd

*"Honor the LORD with your wealth and with
the best part of everything you produce. Then He
will fill your barns with grain, and overflow
your vats with good wine."*

PROVERBS 3:9-10

God's wisdom trumps human wisdom every time. When human wisdom says that hoarding money away will allow us to be rich, God tells us that the more we give, the more we'll receive! After all, money is a stewardship from the Lord. When we honor Him with our money, He trusts us even more! That's why we must turn our hearts toward cheerful giving. We must not fear being charitable with our earnings. There will always be someone who needs it more. Honor the Lord and consider donating to a charity with finances or time. Or, help to fund projects at your local church. Even if it's just with manual labor, a little goes a long way!

September 24th

"Wisdom is more precious than rubies; nothing
you desire can compare with her."

PROVERBS 3:15

We will naturally have many desires in life. God has filled the world with beautiful things, after all! No matter what our hearts long for, we must remember that none is more precious than wisdom. Wisdom will guide us to prosperity in every area of our lives. That's why we must devote ourselves to it. Sure, that new piece of jewelry might look good on us, but wouldn't you trade that for being wise? Think of how infrequently someone describes another person as "wise." It's rare! We must feel blessed that God is sharing His wisdom with us. Now, what will we do with it?

September 25th

"The LORD curses the house of the wicked, but He blesses the home of the upright."

PROVERBS 3:33

We must be careful with how we live, not only for our sake, but for that of our family. When we live sinful and immoral lives, it affects those we love as well. We don't only hurt ourselves, but those who are closest to us. When we are living righteously and at our best, we can care for our loved ones even more. If we won't do it for ourselves, we must be inspired to do it for our family. Once we start living to care for others' needs over our own, we can find increased purpose in our lives. We will look forward to waking up each day, knowing we can better the lives of the people that are special to us.

September 26th

"A fool's proud talk becomes a rod that beats him, but the words of the wise keep them safe."

PROVERBS 14:3

Proud words end up coming back to hurt us. We end up bringing punishment upon ourselves when we speak rashly without thinking! We offend others and end up losing relationships that brought benefits to our lives. Wise words will instead help us to grow spiritually and personally. Aspire to create a safe environment for you and your family. An environment where there is room to grow. Where honesty is placed above all. And where people aren't scared to ask for help when they need it.

September 27th

*"The man who commits adultery is an utter
fool, for he destroys himself. He will be wounded
and disgraced. His shame will never be erased."*

PROVERBS 6:32-33

Sin eats us from the inside out. It erodes our character and
consumes us in every way. This is especially true of adultery.
We must be careful to follow God's design for sexuality, not
desiring anyone other than our spouse. Adultery is serious in
God's eyes, and He will punish it. The same with viewing adult
content on the internet. It may come across as harsh, but that's
the mentality we should have when it comes to infidelity. We
may have moments of weakness from time to time, but always
return to God's desire for us.

September 28th

"Guide a horse with a whip, a donkey with a bridle, and a fool with a rod to his back!"

PROVERBS 26:3

The foolish and lazy of this world will typically not change by mere words or motivation. Sometimes we must be strong in how we approach our conversations with them. If we really need someone to do something, we may have to be brutally honest with them, sharing God's wisdom and warning them of the consequences if they continue to be lazy! If words don't get through to them, examples might. But be cautious that being lazy can be contagious. It's best not to surround yourself with too many of these people. Why waste any day when we are so blessed with all the beauty on this Earth to explore?

September 29th

"Tainted wealth has no lasting value, but right living can save your life."

PROVERBS 10:2

At different times in life, we may find ourselves in situations where we can gain money from unsavory situations. We must be careful not to partake in such sin, because the wealth we receive will be tainted and carry no real value for our lives. Instead, when we choose to do the right thing, we will gain godly character, something money could never bring us. Take the rise of gambling for instance. Sure, this may lead to a fun night out with friends, but it's fleeting. It also has the danger of becoming habitual. It's wiser to take the long route when it comes to building wealth. Keep your business intentions pure along the way and every dollar earned will feel special.

September 30th

"Wise people treasure knowledge, but the babbling of a fool invites disaster."

PROVERBS 10:14

What our hearts treasure reflects our inner character. When we have godly character, we treasure knowledge. That knowledge leads to deep wisdom which in turn leads to a prosperous life. But when we are not careful with our words and shun wisdom, we bring disaster upon ourselves. Our sinful words and actions bring us trouble in life! Sometimes the simplest message can have the most profound impact. That's why it's so easy to relate to the proverbs. They are concise but pack a big punch. We must treasure the teachings available to us in this life and attempt to apply that knowledge.

October 1st

"The godly are showered with blessings; the words of the wicked conceal violent intentions."

PROVERBS 10:6

Parents love to give their children wonderful gifts, time, love, energy, and attention. We enjoy seeing our children happy! God is the same way. He is our loving Father in heaven, and He desires to shower us with blessings. But when we turn away from Him, this isn't possible, and it's our own choice. Turn to God and watch as He rains His blessings down! Start by setting pure intentions for yourself. Examine an area or two that you wish to improve in your life. The first step of any journey is to identify the problem or need. From there, God will guide us on our mission. The road will be full of twists and turns, but it will be fun!

October 2nd

*"People who wink at wrong cause trouble, but a
bold reproof promotes peace."*

PROVERBS 10:10

When we witness sinful actions and do nothing, we silently approve of what is transpiring. In our lack of action, we let these sinful events continue and grow. This can cause great conflict and pain. We must look to help correct these actions and bring the sinful to repentance. If we achieve this, we will be promoting peace and godliness in that situation. This does not mean that we should engage in conflict. We can promote peace by setting strong examples for those around us. Be the calm, well-spoken voice at the table. Be the one, who pauses before responding to hateful words.

October 3rd

"Hatred stirs up quarrels, but love makes up for all offenses."

PROVERBS 10:12

When we harbor negative feelings and hate towards others, it creates fighting and conflict. Even if we have a legitimate reason to be angry, hate never makes anything better. What's best is if we show forgiveness to our offender as Christ shows forgiveness to us. That we can show them love and bring healing to both of our hearts. Choosing to take the high road requires discipline and strength. It may not happen the first time we get into a conflict, but as we bring awareness to choosing to be forgiving, it will become easier over time.

October 4th

*"Hiding hatred makes you a liar; slandering
others makes you a fool."*

PROVERBS 10:18

It's okay to be honest with our feelings. There will be times when we feel hatred in our hearts. That's normal! It happens. What matters is what we choose to do at that moment. Do we harbor that hatred and let it grow? Or do we turn it over to God and choose to be loving instead? Don't be a fool, slandering others and building hatred up in your heart. Trust in God to take it all away and let his wisdom fill you with love instead. The first step is to be aware of the negative emotions when they arise. Acknowledge them but let them pass over you like clouds in the sky. They exist, but we do not have to give in to them.

October 5th

---

*"Too much talk leads to sin. Be sensible and keep
your mouth shut."*

PROVERBS 10:19

There's no need to constantly fill the space in our lives with many words. We must be thoughtful and intentional about the words we speak. If we are not, we can be led to sinful speech. The power of our words is a great responsibility, so it's better to be quiet than to say things you cannot take back! Sitting in silence can be difficult. Especially if we're sharing a space with someone we don't know well. Instead of filling that space with meaningless words, we can try sitting with discomfort. Pay attention to what comes up. What other sensations do you notice?

October 6th

"The blessing of the LORD makes a person rich,
and He adds no sorrow with it."

PROVERBS 10:22

God has different standards to what makes us rich or poor in this life. An abundance of money doesn't make us rich, but a thriving and abundant relationship with God does. Spiritual maturity is the goal to a prosperous life. And getting there is easy: all we must do is follow God! Money can buy us fleeting pleasures that we are convinced we need in the heat of the moment. That doesn't make us rich. That makes us careless with our spending. We should try to count our blessings from within and be grateful for everything we have in life. When we understand how blessed we are and learn to appreciate that, abundance of all forms will enter our lives.

October 7th

"Doing wrong is fun for a fool, but living wisely brings pleasure to the sensible."

PROVERBS 10:23

Living a life of godliness and righteousness is not boring and stuffy as many people claim it is. When we have a thriving relationship with God, we find enjoyment and pleasure in living by His ways! He brings us joy in life and desires that we would have fun! He wants us to enjoy the life and world He created for us. Just as a loving parent wants to see their child enjoy life, so too does God delight in watching us be happy. It's common for people to mock religion in modern society. Why? Believing in a higher power is key to living a fulfilling life! With God's wisdom, we can find meaning in the small things. We can build healthy relationships and lead purposeful lives.

October 8th

"Fear of the LORD lengthens one's life, but the years of the wicked are cut short."

PROVERBS 10:27

When we have a healthy fear and reverence for the Lord, it helps us to make wise decisions. These decisions guide our lives for the better. We are healthier in every aspect and enjoy the blessings that lead to a long, wholesome life. Sinful living will do the opposite, shortening our longevity. The first step to repenting from sin is to recognize it. Then we must feel remorse for them. After that, we can confess what we have done and ask God to forgive us. He will understand. We must be fearful of Him so that we can learn from our sins, forgive them, and live without guilt and shame.

October 9th

"The hopes of the godly result in happiness, but the expectations of the wicked come to nothing."

PROVERBS 10:28

We all have hopes and dreams in life. When we choose to be godly, our hopes are realized, and God brings about the manifestation of our dreams. Yet when we turn away from God, we don't receive the desires of our heart because we have cut ourselves off from blessings by choice. Ultimately, it's up to us! The more we live clean lives, the more blessings we shall receive. Living a clean life starts with turning bad habits into good ones. Maybe we have a habit of being cynical or saying negative things. We can recognize the bad habit, and slowly work on changing it one day at a time.

October 10th

"The way of the LORD is a stronghold to those with integrity, but it destroys the wicked."

PROVERBS 10:29

Think of a stronghold as a fortress of protection that one can use as shelter in times of war. The earth is a spiritual battlefield, but the Lord grants us strongholds in His presence. When we are close to Him, no attack of the enemy can impact us. We will be continually safe in His arms where we belong. Aim to build your personal stronghold high and mighty like medieval castle walls. When times get tough or we fall upon difficult situations in our lives, we can fall back on the fact that we built our strongholds well. The more we seek out God's wisdom, the higher the castle walls become. Even when we make mistakes along the way, we can strengthen those walls by learning from our wrongdoings.

October 11th

"The godliness of good people rescues them; the ambition of treacherous people traps them."

PROVERBS 11:6

Walking in godliness grants us the protection and power of God. In times of great trials, God's influence can save our lives! The joy, contentment, and peace we find in Him can carry us through even the most raging of storms. But when sin is in our hearts and we're far from God, our lack of contentment and continual desire for more traps us and leads to ruin. Anxiety and depression are common in the modern day. It's no wonder why. Community support is at an all-time low. People are skeptical of one another and keep to themselves. We can slowly rid those negative emotions by seeking God's help.

October 12th

"When the wicked die, their hopes die with them, for they rely on their own feeble strength."

PROVERBS 11:7

We are human beings, so that means we have limited strength. God doesn't have that problem. His strength is unlimited and knows no bounds. What's beautiful is that He will not withhold ever using that power on our behalf. That's why we must not live wicked lives, unless we want to be stuck going through life trying to depend on our own limited means to scrape by. If we're experiencing pain, chronic ailments, or negative thoughts we must be active about working on them. It's the same with religion. We must actively work at it to derive more out of it. We may have limited strength, but we must try and maximize what we have, to live the best possible life that we can.

October 13th

"With their words, the godless destroy their friends, but knowledge will rescue the righteous."

PROVERBS 11:9

We have a massive responsibility with the relationships we have been entrusted with in this life. We can either build our friends up or tear them down. If we speak careless words, we will hurt them, destroy their confidence, and ruin our relationship. But if we encourage and empower them, we will help lead them to their full potential. We should never fear someone else's success. When our friends need encouragement, we should give them the best possible advice we know. Helping others succeed in life is equally important as our own successes.

October 14th

"A gossip goes around telling secrets, but those who are trustworthy can keep a confidence."

PROVERBS 11:13

Being trustworthy is a critical aspect of having godly character and maintaining thriving relationships. If we are not trustworthy, we will hurt our friends, gain a bad reputation, and only be able to stay at a surface level with our peers. But being trustworthy will help us to build relationships unlike any we have ever known before. If you've ever struggled to maintain friendships or grow closer with people, it could be due to a lack of trust. Strive to be someone that will always tell the truth, even if it's arduous. Watch your friendships and close relationships blossom when you can be counted on as a reliable source of truth in any situation.

October 15th

"There's danger in putting up security for a stranger's debt; it's safer not to guarantee another person's debt."

PROVERBS 11:15

If we wish to be wise financially and good stewards of God's resources to us, we must not interject ourselves into other people's finances. We are each called to manage our own resources accordingly. When we put ourselves in the middle of another's debt, we put ourselves in danger. Helping someone in need is different than giving someone significant financial assistance and needing it to be paid back. We all have expenses to pay in life, we should prioritize helping our friends and family first and beyond that, give to those in need when able. But leveraging our own security to pay off a random person's debts could cast financial ruin on us too.

October 16th

"Godly people find life; evil people find death."

PROVERBS 11:19

Eternal life is found in God and God alone. We cannot find eternal salvation anywhere else. This makes our decision simple: either we accept the gift of eternal life offered by the sacrifice of Jesus or we push God away and walk the path toward eternal damnation. Some proverbs read harshly. But the message is clear. The more we practice our godly ways, the more enriching our lives will be. We will find meaningful relationships, stable work, fulfilling hobbies and each day will be more enjoyable. When we get away from God and his teachings, evil can creep into our lives and plant seeds that are difficult to get rid of.

October 17th

"The godly can look forward to a reward, while the wicked can expect only judgment."

PROVERBS 11:23

God makes it clear what awaits us in the end times. The Bible doesn't hold back what it says regarding what the fruit of our lives will be depending on the way we choose to live. If we live godly lives, we will receive abundant rewards in heaven and eternal life. Yet if we choose wicked, we should expect judgment and eternal separation from God. The choice is up to us! Begin each day by setting an intention on how to have a meaningful day. Fulfill each intention you set until they become easy to accomplish. Good habits will form. Godly ways will take over. And we will soon be living enriching lives that will lead us to eternity.

October 18th

"The generous will prosper; those who refresh others will themselves be refreshed."

God holds everything in His hand. He has all the power, authority, and influence over our world. Yet, He is generous with it. He grants us innumerable blessings of His own love and free will. In kind, we should follow His example and be generous to others. When we are, we should expect to see God's continual generosity enrich our lives. The more we give, the more we get in return. However, the highest form of giving is unconditional. When we expect nothing in return, we will derive more happiness from the art of giving. Instead of thinking about what you'd like for your birthday, place more emphasis on what someone else would enjoy. Let's stop making life all about us!

October 19th

"If you search for good, you will find favor; but if you search for evil, it will find you!"

PROVERBS 11:27

We will reap the fruit of whatever it is we pursue in this life. If we seek out goodness, love, and peace, we will receive it in kind. But if we seek out evil through living a sinful life, sin will pursue us and overtake us. Choose goodness and let it come to define your life and faith. Resist and refuse evil in all forms. It may present itself in the form of substances, negative people or get rich quick schemes. Be mindful of what endeavors you pursue. Whether it's a new relationship, career, or friendship, make sure it begins with good intentions and not a false sense of belief.

October 20th

"Loyalty makes a person attractive. It is better to be poor than dishonest."

PROVERBS 19:22

Loyalty and honesty are two traits that cannot be replaced in the life of the godly. If we are disloyal and dishonest, we can't have healthy relationships. We also can't be walking in line with God's will, for He commands us to be loyal and honest like Him in everything we do. When we are loyal, our spirits will radiate, and our skin will glow. When we are honest, our bodies will heal, and our minds will think clearly. God values these two traits, because they help us live better lives individually, but they will also benefit everyone else around us. Loyalty and honesty truly make for symbiotic relationships.

October 21st

"A worthy wife is a crown for her husband, but a disgraceful woman is like cancer in his bones."

PROVERBS 12:4

This proverb goes for both husband and wife. When we live up to our end of the marriage and strive to be a godly spouse, we bless our commitment to ourselves, our spouse, and our future family. That's why we must give our all to our marriages. They affect more than just us. We have a family and future generations to bless through our actions. We must not lead them all to ruin. A marriage is an equal compromise of 50 percent from each partner. They each need to pull their own weight and treat the commitment for what it is, sacred. Worthy spouses can add infinite value to our lives, we must not take that for granted and uphold our end of the bargain.

October 22nd

"The plans of the godly are just; the advice of the wicked is treacherous."

PROVERBS 12:5

If we are to lead a spiritually healthy life, we must make sure to surround ourselves and take advice only from the godly. Those who turn away from the Lord have no helpful advice for us unless they turn to repentance. But the advice of the wise and godly will only enrich our path and help us to live out God's divine purpose for our lives. There are many paths to choose in life. Some will feel like an obvious decision at the time, only to lead to a disappointing road. That's okay! There is no shame in adjusting course and finding a new road to travel down. Being spiritually healthy will give our minds plenty of bandwidth to process those choices.

October 23rd

*"Thieves are jealous of each other's loot, but the
godly are well rooted and bear their own fruit."*

PROVERBS 12:12

When we steal and try to take the blessings of others, we
are never satisfied with what we have. Such behavior
comes from a discontent heart. Yet if we live with godly
contentment, we are satisfied with what we have and can be self-
sufficient in godly ways. Then, we won't have to resort to hurting
others to fulfill our own needs. Each day we rise is a blessing. We
must practice gratitude and give thanks to God for the things we
all take for granted in this life. Each cup of coffee, each meal on
the table and a comfortable bed to lay should all be cherished.
The more we appreciate the little things, the less envious of
others' lives we will become.

October 24th

"The wicked are trapped by their own words, but
the godly escape such trouble."

PROVERBS 12:13

When we are careless with our communication and speak in ungodly ways, we deceive ourselves. Through our words, we invite evil into our heart, and it will spread through our lives. If we are careful to avoid this from the beginning, we will never have to worry about it! We can think about a situation where we have felt stuck in life. Maybe it was at work, school or in a relationship. To get unstuck we can use our words. When we communicate clearly and kindly about our needs, we can alleviate the pressures around us and start living better lives.

October 25th

"Wise words bring many benefits, and hard work brings rewards."

PROVERBS 12:14

Wisdom and hard work go hand in hand. One brings about mental and emotional stability while the other meets our physical needs. Together, they help us to achieve our highest goals. Not only that, but they also nourish us spiritually, clearing a path forward to the Lord Himself. If we seek wisdom and work hard, we will reap every benefit imaginable! Picture a scenario where we devoted the next six months to working hard and speaking intelligent words. Where would we end up? Think of how much would be accomplished in that span of time and how much better our lives would look.

October 26th

"Truthful words stand the test of time, but lies are soon exposed."

PROVERBS 12:19

Our God is a god of truth. He hates lies because they hurt and destroy the good He has placed within the world. Truthful words will stand the test of time, enduring far beyond us and building a legacy in the Lord. But our lies will soon be exposed, destroying any good we've accomplished prior and ensuring that our legacy will not live on. The truth will always prevail. Lies will always be found out one way or another. One lie turns into two. Suddenly the story begins to change altogether. Before we know it, we're living a life of lives. We can avoid this by always being truthful and never straying from honesty despite how difficult it may be.

October 27th

"Work hard and become a leader; be lazy and become a slave."

PROVERBS 12:24

There are countless reasons to work hard in life. First, it is our duty as part of whatever community we live in. Each of us brings our own skills and perspective to the table to contribute to the greater good. That hard work also helps us to build wealth that will provide for us and our families. Imagine being able to dictate your future by the choices you make today. Are you satisfied with your current career? If not, work even harder outside of your 9-5 hours to find another way to generate income. If we get too content in our situations, we can run the risk of sitting behind the desk for the rest of our lives, missing out on many worldly experiences.

October 28th

"Lazy people want much but get little, but those who work hard will prosper."

PROVERBS 13:4

Being lazy reaps no rewards for our lives. When we are lazy, we will mourn the things we do not have, even going to the lengths of blaming God Himself. We point our finger everywhere but to ourselves, where the blame really lies. All we must do is rise and put forth the work necessary to build the life we desire. Anything we can imagine, is obtainable. God gave each of us unique gifts to use. We all have a story to tell. We all can dig deep and put in the work required to make significant changes in our lives. If you'd rather be somewhere else at this place and time, you must ask yourself how much harder you can work to get there.

October 29th

*"Trouble chases sinners, while blessings reward
the righteous."*

PROVERBS 13:21

The way we live our lives ultimately catches up with us. Take drinking, for example. At first, it may be fun and spark our social lives. But then it begins to overtake us, making us its slave. Then, everything we thought we gained crumbles, including our relationships. It leaves us with nothing left. In the same way, all our sinful behaviors will eventually steal life and joy from us. Take adult content as another example. It will give us a hit of pleasure initially, but eventually it will end the same way all other substances end: despair. If we can avoid these substances altogether, our self-discipline will inspire confidence in us. If we slip up and occasionally take liberties with these substances, it is okay, but we must seek to do better and be in full control of our desires.

October 30th

"A poor person's farm may produce much food,
but injustice sweeps it all away."

PROVERBS 13:23

Some people in poverty do not bring it upon themselves. They may work hard and bear abundant fruit, only for it to be taken away by injustice. This is not God's doing, but rather the free will of sinful people at work. That's why we must emulate God in every way and seek to fight against every injustice in our world. Sometimes all it takes for someone to lose their hard work is a stroke of bad luck. It can be a fluky event; it can be an act of injustice. Whichever the case, we must keep these people in our prayers. For it could just as easily happen to us. It's another reminder of why we should be grateful for every blessing in our lives.

October 31st

"Those who follow the right path fear the LORD; those who take the wrong path despise Him."

PROVERBS 14:2

Fear of the Lord means reverence, respect, and love for Him. Just as we don't want to disappoint our parents when we are children, the godly don't want to displease God. That path leads us straight to a prosperous life. When we turn from this path, we push God away with our own free will. Even if we are not intending to do so with our words, our actions make our feelings clear. When we act in a positive manner consistently, we are showing our desire to live godly lives. When we think pure and uplifting thoughts, we are on the path to salvation. Continue doing so with a healthy fear of God, and a joyous life will be lived.

November 1st

"Without oxen a stable stays clean, but you need a strong ox for a large harvest."

PROVERBS 14:4

The resources we need to complete our work come with responsibilities themselves. Instead of seeing these responsibilities as trouble and additional work, we must realize how much of a blessing they provide to us. Our responsibilities may be many, but hard work leads to heavenly rewards! Sometimes the more responsibilities we have, the more overwhelmed we feel. That is until we grow and expand from the additional obligations in our lives. The more we must take care of, the more eager we are to get out of bed each morning to get things done. If we continue to bear more responsibility in life, it's a sign that we are on the road to abundance.

November 2nd

"A mocker seeks wisdom and never finds it, but knowledge comes easily to those with understanding."

PROVERBS 14:6

When we are stubborn, sinful, and uncoachable, we will fail to find wisdom. But when we have godly understanding, wisdom will gravitate toward us, and we will find it without looking. Not only that, but it will be much easier to apply it to our lives because we will trust in God and be willing to make whatever changes are necessary. A change can be quite simple if we let it be. Instead of fearing change, it should be embraced. With change comes new opportunities, new people to love and new friends to connect with.

November 3rd

"The prudent know where they are going, but fools are deceived."

PROVERBS 14:8

Being prudent means showing care and thought for the future, preparing accordingly for whatever may come next. We keep our eyes open to many possibilities and trust in the Lord to guide us toward the right path. When we are foolish, we lie to ourselves of what may come without trusting in the Lord's plans for our lives. We wouldn't sign up to run a marathon without training first. Nor would we walk into a big meeting without a plan. The more time we spend preparing, the more we'll be ready for whatever challenge presents itself.

November 4th

"There is a path before each person that seems right, but it ends in death."

PROVERBS 14:12

In our own limited human understanding, we may think we know the best path to go down in life. But if it's not where the Lord is leading us, it will not succeed! We must follow His way. In His infinite wisdom, God is the only one who knows which way is best for us. His intended course for us may have many twists and turns along the way. But we must never lose our faith in His vision for us. We should continue to place our trust in Him and be conscious that each of us shares the same fate. With that in mind, we'll be more motivated to never let a day go to waste.

November 5th

---

*"Children who mistreat their father or chase
away their mother are an embarrassment and a
public disgrace."*

PROVERBS 19:26

God has given us parents to love, guide, and show us His
ways. We must love and respect our parents as emissaries
of God Himself. Even if our parents weren't godly in raising us,
we should still never show them disrespect, but rather pray that
God would open their hearts and place His healing hand upon
their lives. Conversely, if our parents raised us well, it's one of
the biggest blessings we can receive in this life, and we must
aspire to do the same for our children.

November 6th

"Only simpletons believe everything they're told!
The prudent carefully consider their steps."

PROVERBS 14:15

There are many worldviews prevalent in our society today, and people will be vocal about sharing their own. We must be careful then to weigh everything we hear against the standard of God's word, the Holy Bible. If we don't, we will easily be led away by the false doctrines of the world. With the amount of information we consume on a daily basis, we must remain strong willed to never be swayed easily. Everyone in today's world has an agenda for us. We're being pulled in so many ways. But God's teachings will give us the wisdom and guidance we need to tune out all the other noise.

November 7th

"Work brings profit, but mere talk leads to poverty!"

PROVERBS 14:23

We all know someone in our lives who talks a big game but doesn't back it up. We must be diligent not to fall into the same trap. We may convince ourselves and others that we are doing great things, but only putting in the hard work required will bring us the profit we desire! Talking doesn't accomplish much. Taking action does. If we start putting into motion our ideas and work hard to execute our visions, we'll achieve anything we want to accomplish.

November 8th

"A truthful witness saves lives, but a false witness is a traitor."

PROVERBS 14:25

When we are called upon to be a witness toward a particular situation, we must be committed to speaking the truth wholeheartedly. When we give an honest account, we help to resolve the situation in a godly way. False witnesses can ruin someone's life, and then that sin is on us! We must be aware of how much responsibility we are given over someone else's life. Maybe it's a loved one, a friend or a trusted colleague. We owe the people nearest to us to always be faithful and accountable.

November 9th

"Those who fear the LORD are secure; He will be a refuge for their children."

PROVERBS 14:26

Choosing a personal relationship with God gives us the ultimate security in life. He is our Father and will stop at nothing to protect His children. Not only that, but He is all-powerful, and nothing can prevail against Him. We have the blessed opportunity to walk with God throughout every moment of our lives and rest in His divine protection. Don't let that opportunity go to waste! When we are feeling lost or confused about our purpose in life, we should turn to God. His teachings will help us to change our daily habits and get back on our intended path.

November 10th

"Those who oppress the poor insult their Maker,
but helping the poor honors Him."

PROVERBS 14:31

God loves each person on this earth equally and unconditionally. We are all made in His image. The things that determine "success" according to the world hold no relevance in the eyes of God. That's why we must commit ourselves to serving the poor. They are irreplaceable to God and we would honor Him by helping to meet their needs. We can learn just as much from the poor as we can from the rich. Society is a tough critic when it comes to determining who is successful so we must attempt to treat everyone in our daily life as an equal. God created us to live in harmony.

November 11th

---

*"A gentle answer deflects anger, but harsh words
make tempers flare."*

PROVERBS 15:1

There will come a time in our lives when we are in a tense conversation with another person. How we respond to that person will determine how the rest of the situation unfolds. If we respond in anger or hate, tempers will rise, and the conflict will escalate out of control. But if we respond with a loving, gentle answer, then we will be able resolve the conflict in a healthy way. Sometimes it might take us being the bigger person to resolve a conflict. Never be afraid to be a leader when it comes to this. While it might feel glorifying to "win" an argument, it's more dignified to take the higher road.

November 12th

*"The LORD is watching everywhere, keeping
His eye on both the evil and the good."*

PROVERBS 15:3

There is nowhere we can go to escape the watchful eye of the Lord. That's precisely why we must commit to living in godly ways in each of our public and private lives. God sees it all! He holds us accountable to being righteous in every area. Think of some actions that you wish to change in your private life. God will see you attempting to do better and aid you in your quest of betterment. It begins with us acknowledging that we want to change and then attempting to live a godly life with these realizations.

November 13th

"Don't wait in ambush at the home of the godly,
and don't raid the house where the godly live."

PROVERBS 24:15

Plotting any kind of evil against those beloved by God is never a good choice. When we rob, cheat, lie, or deceive anyone God is sorely displeased with us. At the end of the day, we know that it's completely and utterly wrong to harm an innocent person, especially the godly. We must always remember this. Cheating to get ahead will never result in prosperity. Sure, there could be a short-term win experienced, but living a life like this will slowly implode over time.

November 14th

*"For the despondent, every day brings trouble;
for the happy heart, life is a continual feast."*

PROVERBS 15:15

Our attitude will go a long way in determining how our lives play out. If we approach each day with joy, optimism, and a refreshed heart in the Lord, we will see the good things around us. We will enjoy life abundantly! But when we meet each day downcast with a pessimistic heart, we will notice the trouble surrounding us. Even if we face some obstacles during the day like bad traffic, spilled milk or having to stay late at work, we can still choose to have a good attitude and try to see something positive in whatever inconvenience we are faced with.

November 15th

"A hot-tempered person starts fights; a cool-tempered person stops them."

PROVERBS 15:18

Some of us may struggle with our temper, but that's something we can fight against. If we are to live out healthy relationships and be loving toward other people, it's crucial that we learn how to control our temper. Lashing out at others ruins a multitude of things in our lives and causes pain. Instead of reacting to everything, try slowing down and taking some deep breaths. Wait a minute before speaking what you want to say. All it can take to ruin a relationship is a few words, it's not worth it.

November 16th

*"The LORD detests evil plans, but He delights
in pure words."*

PROVERBS 15:26

The posture of our heart is important to God. It breaks His heart to see us plotting things that are sinful and that could hurt other people. He doesn't want us to take shortcuts or undermine anyone else to get ahead in life. He wishes that we would find joy in His presence, being content in the simple yet beautiful things that He created for us. We must turn from evil and run into God's loving arms! There is so much beauty surrounding us in this world. Whether it's nature, good food, or experiencing a new culture through travel, we should soak up the beauty in everyday life.

November 17th

"A cheerful look brings joy to the heart; good news makes for good health."

PROVERBS 15:30

The way we feel emotionally has an impact on how we feel mentally, physically, and spiritually. All these things work in unison to determine our overall health. That's why it's essential that we surround ourselves with godly people, joyful things, and pursuits that the Lord leads us to. When we find joy and peace in life, our health will benefit greatly as well as our spirit! It all starts with a smile. Even if we're having a rough day, we can try smiling. Things will feel a little better. At a certain point, health is wealth. If we can take care of our mind, body, and spirit, we are likely to lead prosperous lives.

November 18th

"If you reject discipline, you only harm yourself;
but if you listen to correction, you grow in
understanding."

PROVERBS 15:32

Sometimes it is hard to hear that we aren't doing something right, but we must change that mindset and be open to transformation in ourselves. When a godly person gives us honest and vulnerable corrections, we will grow and become better if we accept it! If we reject it, we've done no harm to the other person, only to ourselves! Every day is an opportunity to learn something new and grow. Don't let it go to waste! Sometimes it's easier for others to see fault in us. There's valuable information to gain from that.

November 19th

"When people's lives please the LORD, even their
enemies are at peace with them."

PROVERBS 16:7

L iving in a godly way toward everyone has a powerful way of diffusing potential conflicts. When we are peaceful and loving toward others, it can be much more challenging for them to respond with hate. That's why we must reflect Christ to everyone, seeking to meet their needs in any way we can. Life is too short to have enemies. People will make mistakes. People will say things that we don't agree with. Especially in the modern-day world, everyone wants to express their opinions. We can lead by example and not give in to people's attention-seeking behavior.

November 20th

"The LORD demands accurate scales and balances; He sets the standards for fairness."

PROVERBS 16:11

God is fair and just in every way. When we are met with unfairness in this life, we must not consider it to be the doing of the Lord. The world He created is now in the grasp of sin and some people have bad intentions. It is this evil perpetrated by others that causes the unfairness we face. This situation leaves us with an important choice: do we feed the unfairness by treating others in the same way or do we fight against it with love and fairness?

November 21st

"Pride goes before destruction, and haughtiness before a fall."

PROVERBS 16:18

B eing prideful is a dangerous trap. Sometimes we fall into this mindset by accident. It's a good feeling when we work hard and accomplish our tasks, but sometimes it gets to our head! This is dangerous because pride blinds us and changes our character. Humbleness and love go hand in hand, but pride quickly turns us in a more selfish direction. Part of living a spiritual life involves putting others above yourself. Celebrate your partners' accomplishments more than your own. Cook a meal for your loved ones. Do something that shifts the focus off yourself and see how it makes you feel.

November 22nd

Better to live humbly with the poor than to share plunder with the proud."

PROVERBS 16:19

Humble but honest living is more admirable than having riches that were acquired by ungodly means. When we live honestly, we have something more important than any amount of wealth or possessions: deep and godly character. Nothing can replace that, so being humble must be a huge priority in our lives! We consume so much information daily that we get used to seeing others brag about their accomplishments. What does it really matter what someone else has achieved? We all share the same fate. It will age much better if we live a humble and modest life.

November 23rd

"From a wise mind comes wise speech; the words of the wise are persuasive."

PROVERBS 16:23

We have a bigger impact on those in our lives than we could ever imagine. Our words, for better or worse, can change their lives in powerful ways. That's why we must choose wise words in our dealings with others. We can inspire them toward faith in God, which will transform them from the inside out and lead them to eternal life in the Kingdom of God. It feels like a lot of people in today's world are out of touch with spirituality. It doesn't feel like a priority for most people. That's okay. We can't force them to care about religion, but we can share God's wisdom with others. They might relate to it and seek it out themselves.

November 24th

"Without wise leadership, a nation falls; there is safety in having many advisors."

PROVERBS 11:14

While this proverb speaks to the leadership of a nation, it rings true for every aspect of our lives. It's crucial to have wise, godly mentors surrounding us. Their advice, wisdom, and encouragement will help us to thrive in every way! All we must do is listen and apply what they say when appropriate. Think of someone that you respect. It could be a public figure, a coworker, or a friend for example. What about them do you admire? What qualities do they possess that you wish you could implore in your own life? Take some of these qualities and try to implement them into your arsenal.

November 25th

"Those who mock the poor insult their Maker;
those who rejoice at the misfortune of others will
be punished."

PROVERBS 17:5

God has a heart for the poor, plain and simple. He has a passion for seeing them restored to a happy, nourishing, and sustainable way of life. When we insult them or neglect them, we dishonor God Himself. He does not take lightly to such things, and we will not enter His eternal Kingdom if we live this way. Instead, we will face punishment. In this context the "poor" could also be referring to the sick or needy. In any event, taking care of those less fortunate should be one of our top priorities in life and will be a repetitive theme among the proverbs for good reason.

November 26th

"Evil people are eager for rebellion, but they will be severely punished."

PROVERBS 17:11

When sin is living in our hearts, we are eager to find reasons to lash out against the world. This will lead us to rebellion in many different areas of our lives. Sadly, this will lead to our downfall. It is much better to find contentment in the Lord. He will fulfill every one of our needs and leave us with nothing to desire. It's important to do self-reflection to unearth negative emotions we may be harboring. Any negative emotions hiding inside of us can turn into bigger problems that could lead to sin. Check in with yourself and try and understand if there's any hidden resentment hiding beneath the surface.

November 27th

"It is safer to meet a bear robbed of her cubs than to confront a fool caught in foolishness."

PROVERBS 17:12

This is a very interesting proverb. Wouldn't an angry bear be much more dangerous than any person? Absolutely not! While a bear could destroy us physically, if we are godly, our souls will still be saved, and we'll have eternal life. But hanging around the foolish will undermine our character and lead us away from godliness and into eternal damnation. It's a classic tale of "pick your poison." Sure, the bear poses more of a physical threat, but the fool in this proverb can negatively impact you in more ways than just physically.

November 28th

"A friend is always loyal, and a brother is born to help in time of need."

PROVERBS 17:17

God has put many kinds of relationships in our lives, and He calls us to honor them all. God is a communal being Himself, and He made us in His image. That means that relationships are important to Him! They should be important to us as well. That's why we must be loyal to our friends, family, and loved ones. We should be ready to serve them and take care of them in ways that are pleasing to the Lord. Think of some ways that you could improve a current relationship or friendship. What would you change? Slowly try and begin to implement those ideas and be loyal to that relationship.

November 29th

"A cheerful heart is good medicine, but a broken spirit saps a person's strength."

PROVERBS 17:22

Joy is more than an emotion, but rather a state of being that affects us in every way! Joy radiates through us and is contagious to others. Being cheerful can lift our spirits and those of others in powerful ways. The reverse is also true. When we give ourselves over to sorrow, we will lose strength and vibrancy in life. Depression and anxiety will begin to take hold over us. Even if we've had a tough day, we can still try and be positive. We can find little wins along the way and be grateful for our other blessings. This attitude will catch on and be contagious to others, making them want to live in the same way!

November 30th

*"It is wrong to punish the godly for being good
or to flog leaders for being honest."*

PROVERBS 17:26

Sadly, it happens every day: believers are punished for walking by the ways of God. There are still people being martyred around the world for our faith and it is heartbreaking to the Lord. We must pray and fight for our brothers and sisters in Christ. Those who persecute them will find no mercy from God! Even in a more local context, community leaders who try to speak against evil forces are often met with significant criticism. We must never punish someone for being honest. It may just be that we don't like what we're hearing, or that we haven't heard the full story yet.

December 1st

"A truly wise person uses few words; a person with understanding is even-tempered."

PROVERBS 17:27

The more we speak, the more we are trying to fill the air around us. As we say more, the meaning behind our words becomes less. When we are truly wise in the Lord, we get right to the point, using a clear, concise statement to get our message across. Through it all, we keep a cool, calm demeanor no matter what is said. When we attempt to be more understanding, the less we need to say. We can act with loving kindness to comfort the people nearest to us in life.

December 2nd

"Lazy people sleep soundly, but idleness leaves them hungry."

PROVERBS 19:15

When we are lazy, we are content to sleep the days away and worry about the consequences later. But everything we put off today still needs to be done and our tasks will pile up. Before we know it, we will be completely overwhelmed and unable to catch up. If we don't keep up with the work we've been called to do, it will have devastating consequences on our lives. That's why we must commit to working hard in everything! Even if we don't have much going on, we should get off the couch and get moving! Our bodies will thank us.

December 3rd

---

*"Wise words are like deep waters; wisdom flows
from the wise like a bubbling brook."*

It's amazing to think of how deep the ocean is. It goes down
and down for miles, with many wonders to explore and
unearth. Some of the deep-sea creatures are still unknown! It is
this way with the wisdom of God as well. We could continually
plunge into its depths and never reach the bottom. No matter
how much we drink of it, it will continue to nourish our lives.
There's so much to be discovered still. Starting with the proverbs
is a great way to avoid sin in our lives. But there's plenty more to
be discovered.

THE DAILY PROVERBS | 339

December 4th

*"Rumors are dainty morsels that sink deep into
one's heart."*

PROVERBS 18:8

Rumors may seem innocent or unimportant, but they are anything but that. Rumors don't go away easily or quietly. People latch onto them and spread them, hurting others, and destroying their reputations. If we are to live godly lives, we must never spread them. With the prominence of social media, rumors spread like wildfire. Instead of getting stuck in an infinite consumption loop, try and put your phone down for the day. Consume less! The fewer rumors we hear and the less social media we consume, the more capacity our minds will have to think.

December 5th

---

*"The human spirit can endure a sick body, but
who can bear a crushed spirit?"*

PROVERBS 18:14

While physical health and taking care of our bodies is crucial, it's even more important that we take care of ourselves spiritually. Yes, God has given us our bodies as sacred vessels of our souls, but our bodies are temporary while our souls are eternal. If we are healthy spiritually, we will endure until we receive eternal life in God's Kingdom. Even if we have fallen behind on our workout routines or have been too busy to attend that yoga class, we can still practice spirituality. Take a few moments to reflect on what godly wisdom you have learned and be grateful for it.

December 6th

"Flipping a coin can end arguments; it settles disputes between powerful opponents."

PROVERBS 18:18

There are many times in life that no amount of conversation can end a dispute or argument. In times like these, if both solutions are viable and honest, a metaphorical resolution like flipping a coin can be a wise tactic. It means that despite the outcome, there must be compromises on both sides. Otherwise, neither side will come to a mutual agreement. Compromise doesn't mean surrendering your morals, it's simply a way to suggest that each opponent has something good to offer. We must try to strike a balance between both and live in harmony among each other.

December 7th

"Wise words satisfy like a good meal; the right words bring satisfaction."

PROVERBS 18:20

Wise words bring nourishment to the body, mind, and soul. They cast away anxiety, sadness, and anger, instead replacing them with knowledge, peace, and love. The benefits of God's wisdom are endless in our lives! If we choose to chase after the wisdom of God, we will always be satisfied and content, no matter what the world may bring. If we've gone through a rough patch recently, try changing your self-talk to a kinder tone. Tell yourself some of the things you love most about yourself and replace the sadness with happiness!

December 8th

"The tongue can bring death or life; those who love to talk reap the consequences."

PROVERBS 18:21

There are some people who love to talk. Sadly, the talk is not always edifying or upright, rather leading into gossip, rumors, and other ungodly speech. This ends up turning against them, making others not want to be around them, destroying their relationship with God, and bringing the anger of others upon them. It's important to be a clear and honest communicator. But many times, less is more when it comes to conversations. Say what you need to say and then listen! We will learn far more from listening to others than hearing ourselves talk.

December 9th

"Enthusiasm without knowledge is no good; haste
makes mistakes."

PROVERBS 19:2

It's good to be passionate about the things we are doing in life. Passion in its right place can motivate us to accomplish incredible things. But we must ensure that our passion is coupled with wisdom and solid planning. If we rush into something, even with passion behind it, we will not accomplish it as smoothly as we would otherwise! Take your time to do something the right way. Don't give it 50 percent, give it everything you've got. But do so in a manner that you don't burn out along the way.

December 10th

"Many seek favors from a ruler; everyone is the friend of a person who gives gifts!"

PROVERBS 19:6

When we live life with godly wisdom, we live in a prosperous way. When we live successful lives, we can bless the lives of others. This is a beautiful blessing and one that shows good stewardship of God's gifts in our lives. It will bring us many friends and close relationships in which we can share the love of Jesus. The more thoughtful gifts we give, the more others will desire to be around us. It's our way of showing we can think of others more than ourselves. What would that special someone in your life really enjoy receiving? Give it to them!

December 11th

"To acquire wisdom is to love yourself; people who cherish understanding will prosper."

PROVERBS 19:8

Pursuing godly wisdom in life is a practice of self-love. It draws out the full potential that God has placed within us from the beginning. So, when we chase it, we are devoting ourselves to becoming everything God has asked us to be. This is what it means to truly love ourselves while still being humble. The more kind and forgiving we are to ourselves, the more we will be able to be the same for others. It all starts within! If we are unsettled or not living the life that we want, we must change it by loving ourselves first, all good things will follow.

December 12th

"A just king gives stability to his nation, but one who demands bribes destroys it."

PROVERBS 29:4

Leaders play important roles in all our lives. Whether it be at church, home, or in the government, leaders shape our lives in many ways. That's why it's important that we set the example in our own leadership positions and maintain integrity always. Bribes and other common dishonest faults will only hurt others. Sadly, it's far too common for public figures to be involved with bribery and dishonesty today. Pay no means to them! Pity them for they are fools. The best we can do is to walk with God. Live by His word and love one another.

December 13th

"Hot-tempered people must pay the penalty. If you rescue them once, you will have to do it again."

PROVERBS 19:19

Saving people from the consequences of their actions is not always a wise thing. Many sinful people will take that opportunity to simply go sin once again. They will not take it as a blessing and change their ways. Usually, someone that needs to be rescued once, will need help again. And again. And so on until you realize that they are the only ones that can save themselves. Pray for them, but don't get swept away in their habitual cycle.

December 14th

"Get all the advice and instruction you can, so you will be wise the rest of your life."

PROVERBS 19:20

Some people may think that their youth is wasted in the pursuit of knowledge and wisdom, but that couldn't be further from the truth! The sooner we build up a foundation of godly wisdom in our lives, the more it will come to serve us. We will continue to build upon that foundation throughout our lifetime. Read books. Write poetry. Travel. Spend time in nature. Learn more about God. These are all examples of how to get the best instruction you can. Seek more wholesome activities and you'll be rewarded with wisdom and knowledge of a lifetime.

December 15th

---

*"Many will say they are loyal friends, but who
can find one who is truly reliable?"*

PROVERBS 20:6

During the fallen world in which we live, good, reliable
friends can seem like a rarity. This is sad, but true. That's
why when we do find these kinds of friends, we must be fiercely
loyal and loving to them. We must never take them for granted
and do everything we can to see that friendship blossom into its
full potential. It's better to have one or two close friends than it
is to have a big group of acquaintances. There will be few
opportunities in life to meet true and loyal friends. We all know
right away when we've found one. Cherish them and treat them
well.

December 16th

"A false witness will not go unpunished, and a liar will be destroyed."

PROVERBS 19:9

There are few things that upset the Lord more than dishonesty. Lying only hurts others and promotes selfishness. God does not deal kindly with such sins. While repentance will save us, unrepentant lying could lead to our downfall. God will offer us forgiveness, but we must seek that mercy and work toward change in our own hearts. Lying includes being dishonest to ourselves too. Who are we kidding, we all make mistakes. We don't have to lie about them. We can own up to our sins and take accountability for our actions. That is a far better route than being a liar.

December 17th

"Throw out the mocker, and fighting goes, too.
Quarrels and insults will disappear."

PROVERBS 22:10

The company we keep can make or break our lives. When we hang around with people who let their tempers get the better of them, we repeatedly find ourselves involved in drama. If the person will not listen to reason, it's best to surround ourselves with people who will. Then we will no longer be held back by constant fighting and negativity around us. The more distractions and negativity we have in our lives, the less we can produce. When we aren't producing, we are endlessly consuming. Stop the endless feedback loops that drama creates and surround yourself with positive influences.

December 18th

"A person who gets ahead by oppressing the poor or by showering gifts on the rich will end in poverty."

PROVERBS 22:16

Many people have the mentality of getting ahead by any means necessary. This is not godly and is outright evil. Exploiting others will never lead to true wealth but only a life of evil and a degradation of one's own character. We must only build wealth by honest means. Start with a venture that you genuinely believe will help others. Even if it's a service you charge for, make sure your customer is receiving the fair end of the bargain. Never set out with bad intentions for any venture in life. It will come back to bite us.

December 19th

"The wise are mightier than the strong, and those with knowledge grow stronger and stronger."

PROVERBS 24:5

True strength is not about being physically stronger than others or holding more influence over them. Real strength is about being wise. Wisdom will carry us through so much more than the worldly definition of strength ever could. The more we gain knowledge in the Lord, the stronger we become! Sure, it's a good idea to spend time in the gym making us physically tougher. But it's even more valuable to consistently gain knowledge to make ourselves mentally wiser.

December 20th

"He who guards your soul knows you knew. He will repay all people as their actions deserve."

PROVERBS 24:12

Have you ever heard the phrase, "You reap what you sow?" It's farming language, but it means that we get what our actions have brought upon us. This is a true saying. At the time of judgment, God will repay each person for what they have done in this life. How do you want God to view you? What do you need to change in your life today? Think of a few bad habits you have and write down a few suggestions on how to change them. Realize you can easily be free from any evils once you stop giving power to them. Ask for God's help. He will listen.

December 21ˢᵗ

"Trustworthy messengers refresh like snow in summer. They revive the spirit of their employer."

PROVERBS 25:13

It's hard to find trustworthy people to join us in our work, no matter what it is we are doing. Most people are seeking their own self-interests and don't care about accomplishing a mutual mission. But when we find those people, we must reward them for their loyalty and do everything we can to keep them with us because they are immensely valuable to our work. It's the same in relationships. With so many fish in the sea, how do we know who to trust? Use your intuition to guide you. God will bring valuable people into our lives when we are living with pure intentions.

December 22nd

"Don't visit your neighbors too often, or you will wear out your welcome."

PROVERBS 25:17

Hospitality is a godly virtue and one we should practice. But there is also much to be said about maintaining healthy boundaries. Remember, throughout the Gospels, even Jesus took time for solitude! We must respect the boundaries of our family, friends, and peers. Doing so will show true, godly love for them and selflessness on our part. Besides, we all need time to ourselves. Even if we're extroverts! Take some time to be by yourself and see what comes up. Maybe some unwanted thoughts or feelings will present themselves to be addressed.

December 23rd

---

*"Telling lies about others is as harmful as hitting
them with an ax, wounding them with a sword,
or shooting them with a sharp arrow."*

PROVERBS 25:18

L ies are not something to joke around about. That's exactly why the Bible uses such strong language against them! They hurt others beyond what we could imagine. Lies can crush the feelings of others, their self-esteem, and reputation. That's why we must always commit ourselves to honesty. Doing so will please God. In our relationships, we must be a source of truth. No matter the conversation, we must answer in honest ways. The more honest we are, the more sincerity we will attract in return.

December 24th

"Putting confidence in an unreliable person in times of trouble is like chewing with a broken tooth or walking on a lame foot."

PROVERBS 25:19

Chewing with a broken tooth or walking on a lame foot would be painful and counterproductive. The same is true of putting our confidence in an unreliable person. We likely won't get the task at hand completed and it will be painful in the process. If there's anyone unreliable in your life, it might be time to move on from that friendship or relationship. Conversely, if you have just one reliable friend or loved one, possibilities are infinite for what you can accomplish.

December 25th

"Singing cheerful songs to a person with a heavy heart is like taking someone's coat in cold weather or pouring vinegar in a wound."

PROVERBS 25:20

It's okay to mourn and grieve. In fact, it's healthy when done appropriately and in the name of the Lord. If someone is still in that phase of their healing process, it's best that we give them the time and space they need to heal. We can mourn and grieve beside them, but too much of trying to cheer them up will only make them feel worse. It's better to match the energy of the person grieving in effort to show genuine sympathy. Christmas is a day to celebrate with family so let's count all of our blessings. But let's also keep praying for those that might be struggling today.

December 26th

"A proverb in the mouth of a fool is like a thorny branch brandished by a drunk."

PROVERBS 26:9

Imagine a drunk coming after you with a thorny branch. Sounds frightening, doesn't it? Proverbs in the mouth of fools are just as dangerous. Why? Because since they don't understand them, they will trust and spin them for their own purposes. This only results in confusion and the spreading of false beliefs. It's a reminder to be careful where you seek your advice from and where you spend the most time consuming from. Be wary of what certain people have to say, instead place your trust in the godly.

December 27th

"A quarrelsome person starts fights as easily as hot embers light charcoal or fire lights wood."

PROVERBS 26:21

We've all seen how quickly fire can spread when it hits wood. It's both amazing and terrifying at the same time. It's the same way with someone prone to anger and fighting. Their fiery temper can light the flames of conflict quicker than anything we've ever seen. It's much better to work toward peace with everyone. Loving and kind words will have the opposite result in our relationships. We would be wise to commit to them. The holiday season is a time when relatives spend more time than normal together. This can cause some conflicts. Try to be above any arguments that arise by taking the higher road.

December 28th

"An open rebuke is better than hidden love!"

PROVERBS 27:5

While we may feel defensive at first, we must realize that a godly correction or rebuke is a blessing! It helps us to realize things in ourselves we may not have noticed that can bring us closer to God. It's so much better to give and receive these types of corrections than to harbor hidden feelings that will impact others in no way, shape, or form. We must not be offended if someone disagrees with us. Maybe they have a point! The more we listen, the more we will learn.

December 29th

"Just as Death and Destruction are never
satisfied, so human desire is never satisfied."

PROVERBS 27:20

Evil ravages through our world, claiming countless people in its wake. It seems as if evil only continues to grow, never satisfied with what it's taken. Our human desire is the same way, we can get everything we've asked for, and still not be satisfied. The feeling of needing more, creates a large void within us. We will constantly seek to fill it with mind-numbing distractions like social media, alcohol, or other vices. That's why we must turn back toward the image of God within us, choosing to be satisfied in God's providence rather than the fulfillment of our worldly desires. Be wary of trying to "fill the void" with anything but knowledge and wisdom.

December 30th

"To reject the law is to praise the wicked; to obey the law is to fight them."

PROVERBS 28:4

When we reject God's ways, we are simply taking up arms for the forces of the devil. Even if we don't outwardly say it or have that intention, that's exactly what we've done! There is no middle ground in this battle between light and darkness. That's why we must follow God's ways. That's how we stand up against the forces of evil in our world! We must reject any notion that goes against living a godly life. Yes, we all make mistakes. But we can still align our priorities and behaviors to mimic a godly life.

December 31ˢᵗ

"A wise servant will rule over the master's disgraceful son and will share the inheritance of the master's children."

PROVERBS 17:2

This verse teaches us that social status will let us avoid the fate of laziness. If we work hard, we will reap rewards. If we are lazy, we will struggle with the consequences from our lack of effort. We shouldn't look toward others to rescue us from what our idleness has brought upon us, but rather within ourselves and to the Lord for the strength we need to work hard! The new year is a common time for people to attempt to change their lives. There's nothing wrong with that. Just do your best to follow through on the changes you want to set, and not take the lazy route. Imagine how much you will progress in just a few months if you stick with it!

Made in the USA
Coppell, TX
13 March 2023